THE UNITED STATES OF EPIC FAILS

52 Crazy Stories and Blunders Through History
That You Didn't Get Taught in School

BILL O'NEILL

ISBN: 978-1-64845-084-6

DON'T FORGET YOUR FREE BOOKS

GET THEM FOR FREE ON
WWW.TRIVIABILL.COM

CONTENTS

INTRODUCTION

It's a fact that America loves a winner. Whether it's successful military generals, scientists, entrepreneurs, political leaders, or even athletes and sports teams, there's no doubt that Americans like to see success stories.

And there are plenty of success stories throughout American history, beginning with the successful American Revolution, the creation of the government, and nearly 250 years of inventions, innovations, and numerous other victories and high points.

But mixed in with all those countless American success stories have been some pretty epic fails!

In *The United States of Epic Fails: 52 Crazy Stories and Blunders Through History That You Didn't Get Taught in School* you'll read about some of the strangest, funniest and most mind-boggling failures from American history. This book covers the most epic fails in entertainment, sports, government, pop culture, and just about anything else you can think of that happened in the United States.

Some better-known fails - such as the Chicago fire, *Exxon Valdez* tragedy, and 1984 presidential election - are covered in this book, but with an emphasis on what made those fails so epic, and at times unique. You'll read about these historic fails

1

from a perspective that you won't get in most history books, and you surely didn't get in your history classes in high school or college.

Most of the failures you'll read about in this book, though, are ones you've either never heard about, or heard very little about, because, well, everyone involved would like nothing more than to forget about them!

You'll read about some pretty big failures in the entertainment business, such as the TV shows *Turn-On* and *Cavemen*, which executives - for different reasons - decided to green light despite objections from many people.

Some failed individuals are also profiled in this book, including Bud Dwyer, a failed corrupt politician who went out with a bang; Frank Collin, a Jewish neo-Nazi; and Henry Wallace, a presidential candidate who thought running on a pro-Joseph Stalin platform was a good idea.

You'll also read about failed video games, cars, and even two very deadly children's toys - Jarts and the Atomic Energy Laboratory - that were actually quite popular before people realized how dangerous they were.

So, sit back, relax, and enjoy these failures like never before! Remember, for every success that went into making this country great, there were at least a dozen failures.

Here are 52 of them!

1

THE PLUMBERS WHO WEREN'T MASTER SPIES

You have probably read about President Richard Nixon's Watergate scandal in the early 1970s, which brought down his presidency and caused him to resign in 1974. Unfortunately, what Nixon did or didn't do is still somewhat shrouded in mystery since he did resign, and also because many of his top guys who did the dirt for him kept their mouths shut.

Nixon's group of dirty tricksters were a collection of CIA assets and right-wing Cubans who were led by a lawyer named G. Gordon Liddy. Liddy and his band of operatives called themselves the "Plumbers" because they "fixed leaks" in Nixon's White House, but as much as those guys thought they were some sort of super spies, they were failed losers when it came to espionage.

When Nixon became president in 1968, he inherited a heap of domestic and international problems: there were social riots, the Vietnam War was raging, and the economy was unstable. Because Nixon's hold on power was contingent upon many of these social and geopolitical currents, he was constantly paranoid and felt that he needed to "play dirty" to get re-elected in 1972.

So, he hired lawyer G. Gordon Liddy to lead his re-election bid. Nixon gave Liddy plenty of freedom, which led to Liddy using "dirty tricks" to put the president's opponents in uncompromising positions. In reality, most of the tricks failed, but none more so than the May 28 and June 17, 1972 break-ins of the Democratic National Committee (DNC) in the Watergate Office Building in Washington, D.C.

Liddy, together with fellow Plumbers E. Howard Hunt and James McCord, arranged a team of burglars to break into the DNC offices, photograph important files (remember this was 1972 so most information was kept on paper), and place wiretaps. It all sounded like something out of an Ian Fleming or Tom Clancy novel, but in reality, it was amateur hour.

The crew Liddy sent to do the deed, *did* place listening devices in the office on May 28, but their main target was DNC chairman Larry O'Brien. The problem was the wiretap they put on O'Brien's phone didn't work, so the crew had to return to the scene of the crime on June 17.

That should've been the first sign to all involved that this operation was destined for failure.

As the crew was going through the offices on June 17, a security guard noticed there were strips of tape placed over several door latches. The Plumbers did this so they could more easily enter the rooms without having to break into them each time. This ploy made sense at first, but upon further thought, it just shows how woefully unprepared they were and how little training they really had in the world of espionage or crime.

The guard removed the tape strips, but when he did his rounds sometime later, he noticed new tape strips were on the door latches, so he called the police.

Another Plumber, Alfred Baldwin, was supposed to be watching things from a motel room across the street, where he could communicate with the burglars via radio if something was happening…except he was too busy watching a movie!

The four burglars were arrested, and they quickly gave up the rest of the Plumbers. Although Liddy never testified against Nixon or anyone else, the fiasco was enough to end the Nixon presidency.

Today, most people know about Nixon's scandals but often overlooked are the failed losers known as the 'Plumbers'.

2

SOME PEOPLE THOUGHT
THE USFL WAS A GOOD IDEA

Today, in the United States "gridiron" football is the most popular sport and the National Football League (NFL) is the number one league.

But it wasn't always that way.

Baseball ruled the roost of American sports for decades and is still considered "America's pastime." By the 1980s, however, football had eclipsed it in fan interest and overall revenue, so much so that New Orleans entrepreneur David Dixon decided to start a professional league to rival the NFL.

Dixon called his league the United States Football League (USFL).

When the USFL finally began playing games in the spring of 1983, it made quite a big splash in the sports world. The league began with 12 teams that were owned by some pretty big names, including future President Donald Trump, who owned the New Jersey Generals.

The USFL also secured TV rights in local markets as well as for select games to be televised nationally on ABC. And although some teams had initial problems landing homes in stadiums, play began with the games being relatively well-attended and watched on TV.

A big reason for the USFL's initial success was a combination of its novelty and the big-name players that it was able to draft and woo away from the NFL with large contracts. Doug Flutie, Jim Kelly, and Hershel Walker were three of the biggest names USFL teams were able to draft right out of college, while NFL veterans such as Brian Sipe and Gary Barbaro also tried their luck in the upstart league.

But by the second year of play, it became clear to many that the USFL was doomed to be an epic failure.

The high contracts that were being paid for the league's stars combined with smaller than expected revenue led to teams regularly filing bankruptcy and moving locations. Dixon originally proposed a salary cap for each team, which may have helped the solvency issue, but it was never followed.

But the biggest fail was when the owners decided to move the schedule to the fall to compete directly with the NFL.

Although the USFL owners, led by Trump and Chicago Blitz owner Eddie Einhorn, thought the move was a good idea, it was primarily business-based. They hoped to pressure the NFL to merge their teams and build a more lucrative super league.

Their calculation was way off the mark.

The TV networks and stadium shut the USFL out of fall play, so the owners responded with an anti-trust lawsuit.

A federal court ruled in the USFL owners' favor but only awarded them $3.76 in damages. And by that time the damage had already been done, with most of the USFL teams declaring bankruptcy and all the top talent signing contracts with either the NFL or the Canadian Football League (CFL).

Many people look back at the USFL as a case of "what could've been," but the reality is that it was one of the biggest sports fails in American history.

3

BIG DIG OR BIG FAIL?

America the beautiful is full of many architectural wonders. The Hoover Dam, the Empire State Building, and the Space Needle are just a few of the many modern achievements of American engineers and construction workers.

But what about the Central Artery/Tunnel Project (CA/T)???

Chances are unless you're from the Northeast, you don't know what the CA/T is, and even then, you probably know it by its more colloquial name, the "Big Dig." Though the Big Dig was very much a modern architectural project, it paled in comparison to the previously mentioned wonders and is considered by many to be nothing more than a big fail....!

If you're familiar with Boston, Massachusetts then you know that it's an old city (by American standards) that was built long before automobiles were even thought about. The streets are narrow and sometimes seem to go nowhere, so when the Interstate Highway system began being built in the 1950s, state and federal officials had to come up with a way to efficiently bring heavy traffic in and out of the city.

The first idea was elevated freeways, but when that proved to be inadequate, the idea of tunnels was proposed. The plan called for Interstate 93 to run underneath downtown in a 1.5-mile tunnel and for Interstate 90 to run in a 1.6-mile tunnel under part of Boston Bay to connect to Logan International Airport. Once the state received funding, the ground was broken for the project in 1991, but from that point on, it was a comedy of errors.

Work moved slowly when it moved at all and was marked by constant delays and price overruns. Substandard materials were used and although the engineering was sound, it wasn't always executed by the book. Heavy-handed union tactics and corruption were a major part of the problem, which perhaps should've been expected in a city known for organized crime and corruption, but local politics and a healthy dose of "not in my neighborhood" also played a role.

In the end, the Big Dig as it came to be called was "completed" in 2007 for $8 billion. The total represented an incredible 190% overrun and with interest it will cost more than $22 billion and won't be able to be paid off until 2038 or likely never at all.

So, did the people at least get their money's worth?

Well, that remains to be seen, but there have been numerous problems.

Part of the I-90 Tunnel, known as the Ted Williams Tunnel, collapsed in 2006, killing a passenger, and in 2011, there were several leaks in the I-93 Tunnel, the Thomas O'Neil Tunnel, that forced it to be shut down.

It's probably safe to say that when you consider the cost, problems, and price tag of the Big Dig, it was clearly one of America's biggest, if not the biggest, engineering architectural fails.

4

E.T. WAS A GREAT MOVIE, BUT THE VIDEO GAME SUCKED

No matter your age, chances are you've seen the 1982 blockbuster film *E.T. the Extra-Terrestrial*. Despite featuring an alien, the story was really about a boy who befriended and helped a stranger (E.T.). The movie was well-written, featured good acting, and had some fairly good special effects for that era.

The movie spawned E.T. toys and stuffed animals, posters, trading cards, and even a video game.

The video game, though, turned out to be one of the biggest gaming fails in American history.

Released months after the summer blockbuster film, in time for the Christmas season, *E.T. the Extra-Terrestrial* video game for the Atari 2600 home video game console system proved to be such an epic commercial failure that it is cited as one of the reasons for the 1983 home video game crash. Atari lost millions on the game due to its high production costs and nearly three million unsold units.

So why was E.T. such a big fail..?

Atari spent up to $25 million for the rights to the game and had some of their best designers working on it, but they rushed it into production. The company did not undertake trials, which would have told them that the graphics sucked (even for 1982) and the gameplay was confusing.

Take it from me personally - it wasn't the type of game that most 10-year-olds with a low attention span liked.

Although E.T. was an adventure game - the object was to play as E.T., collecting a number of pieces so he could "phone home". There were other adventure games on the market, such as Pitfall! and Raiders of the Lost Ark that had better graphics and playability. E.T. the character may have appealed to 10-year-olds, but the game didn't.

In fact, although sales were at first brisk, many people brought the game back to the store after seeing how bad it was.

The game set Atari back further financially, after it had already faced problems after the release of its 5200-console system (we'll get to that failure a bit later), back to the point where it had a difficult time recovering. After burying many of the unsold games in a landfill in New Mexico, Atari reported $563 million in losses in 1983. Much of those losses had to do with competition from other companies, such as Intellivision and Coleco, and the subsequent collapse of the home video game industry, but there's no doubt that the epic fail of E.T. the video game played its role Atari's demise.

Atari continued as a video game company, but it was a shadow of its former self.

5

BUD DWYER: FAILING IN LIFE AND IN DEATH

It's a fact of life that in our modern world politics and corruption go hand-in-glove. The US probably isn't any better or worse than many industrialized nations in this regard, although there are some unique elements to American political corruption.

Organized crime has historically played a role in American political corruption, and in some states, graft and nepotism are just a way of life. For most politicians, corruption is a very grey area and most of the shady deals they make aren't any different from those their corrupt colleagues make.

And get away with it.

But sometimes a corrupt politician fails with his graft and he makes history - or infamy.

Robert Budd Dwyer, known by his friends, colleagues, opponents, and constituents as Budd, was a Pennsylvania politician who served as a state representative and then as a state senator during the 1970s before being elected as the state's treasurer from 1981 to 1987.

When it came to being a politician, Dwyer was moderately successful. But when it came to being a crook, he was a major failure, although he definitely made sure to leave his mark on the world.

Dwyer's problems came when he accepted bribes from a company the state awarded a contract to for an audit. Many of State of Pennsylvania workers overpaid on their taxes in the 1970s, so the state agreed to pay them back.

It was Dwyer's job to hire a firm to conduct the audit, but he and many of his associates apparently used the opportunity as a personal piggy bank.

This was corruption on a major level, so not only was it revealed, but the powers that be had to make an example of Dwyer and his accomplices. They all began turning on each other and although Dwyer denied any and all involvement in the corruption, a jury found him guilty on December 18, 1986, of 11 counts of felony conspiracy, mail fraud, perjury, and racketeering.

The leaders of Dwyer's Republican Party quickly threw him under the bus and as his sentencing approached, he appeared to be headed to federal prison for a long time.

But as bad as this epic fail in political corruption was, it got a whole lot worse on January 22, 1987.

On that morning, Dwyer gave a press conference at his office in the state capital of Harrisburg, where he proclaimed his innocence and rambled on about how he wasn't resigning.

He then pulled a .357 magnum pistol from a manila envelope and said, "Please, please leave the room if this will...if this will affect you."

Dwyer then gave people a few seconds to leave the room before he placed the monster of a gun barrel in his mouth and pulled the trigger, decorating the wall behind him with his brains.

Budd Dwyer's turn at being a corrupt politician ended in abysmal failure, but his death will never be forgotten.

6

THE FAILURE OF CAMELS
IN THE US ARMY

Yes, you read that correctly, camels, the cute but goofy-looking beasts of burden from the Middle East, were used by the US Army for a brief period in the mid-1800s. So why did this program happen in the first place and why did it become a complete failure?

By the 1840s, the United States was following a philosophy known as "Manifest Destiny," where most Americans - government leaders as well as average people - believed that it was the nation's destiny to conquer the entire continent.

There were two problems with that idea.

The first is that there were plenty of people already there who didn't subscribe to the idea of Manifest Destiny. The sheer number of Americans, though, which was augmented by European immigration, along with superior technology, was enough to keep pushing the Indian tribes westward and onto reservations.

But the second problem was even bigger - the environment.

After you get past the Great Plains and the Rocky Mountains, you encounter a vast desert that runs north-south from Mexico pretty much to the Canadian border, and east-west from the Rockies to the West Coast mountain ranges. Horses, mules, and even oxen weren't always a reliable way to make it across the desert, so the Army brass looked to the Middle East, and Australia, for inspiration.

The British had imported camels into their colony of Australia to explore that land's vast deserts. For the most part, the importation of camels to Australia was a success and even today there is a sizable population of wild/feral camels roaming the Outback. So based on the success in Australia, some in the United States thought a similar program could be done in North America.

The major proponent of the program was Major Henry C. Wayne, who had a difficult time getting any support from the government for his idea. Most thought the idea was silly and quite costly; after all, he'd have to travel to the Middle East to purchase the camels and would also have to bring back drivers since no Americans were familiar with the exotic beasts.

After being turned down at different levels, Wayne finally found a sympathetic ear in 1853 with Secretary of War Jefferson Davis. Yes, *that* Jefferson Davis who would later become the Confederacy's first and only president.

Once Wayne acquired the funding and resources from Davis, he sailed to the Middle East where he made several stops, eventually acquiring 33 camels: two Bactrians (two-hump camels), 29 dromedaries (one-hump camels), a dromedary calf, and a dromedary-Bactrian mix. He also hired expert camel drivers, which included a Syrian-Greek man named Hi Jolly.

17

When the motley crew finally arrived in the United States, they reported to Camp Verde, Texas, which would become the home base of the US Camel Corp.

The Camel Corp did two major reconnaissance missions of Texas and the southwestern territories in 1857 and 1859, and by all accounts, it did well in the desert conditions. However, then a couple of things happened that led to its failure.

Well, one major thing.

When the American Civil War broke out Texas joined the Confederacy and the Camel Corp fell into the rebels' hands. The Confederacy had bigger problems than what to do with the Camel Corp, and not having anyone who knew how to work with the animals, they let the program lapse.

After the Union won the war and Texas was brought back into the fold, the Camel Corp wasn't restarted. The fact that Jefferson Davis was associated with its creation definitely had something to do with that, but other considerations probably played bigger roles.

There just weren't enough men around who knew how to drive and care for camels, and perhaps more importantly, there just weren't enough men who *wanted* to deal with the strange beasts. Manifest Destiny was carried out by men on horses, not camels, so for most Americans in the West, the camel was just too foreign. Americans could handle riding mules or even donkeys, but not camels.

Besides, in the years immediately after the Civil War, industrialists were using their capital to connect California to the rest of the US via railroads. The march of technological progress proved to be the final and biggest factor that made the US Camel Corp one of the biggest failures in American military history.

7

LIP SYNCING THEIR
WAY TO FAILURE

If you're under the age of 40, there's a good chance you don't know much about, or maybe have never even heard of, the most epic music fail in American history. Those of you who do remember, or possibly forgot, will be reminded by these two words: Milli Vanilli.

Yes, Milli Vanilli, the strangely-named Euro-pop band that came on the American music scene in 1989 with their platinum album, *Girl You Know It's True*, which produced three number one songs on the *Billboard* Hot 100.

For about a year, everywhere you went, it was Milli Vanilli. They were on MTV constantly; received nonstop play on Top 40, pop, and R&B radio stations; and were the subject of numerous interviews.

Milli Vanilli was definitely quite different from what Americans were used to at the time.

It was basically a two-man group of Fab Morvan, a French-born dancer and musician of Caribbean ancestry, and Rob

Pilatus, who was also a dancer and musician but was of African American and German ethnicity. The two men really didn't look like black American musicians of the era, with their long braids and Euro-style clothing, nor did they sound like it. Both men had heavy European accents and didn't speak English very well.

That last part should have been the first clue to the imminent failure.

But as Milli Vanilli kept charting hit after hit, they were also recognized by their peers in the music industry with a Grammy Award for the best new artist in 1990 and three American Music Awards that year.

But it was all a big charade.

Although Morvan and Pilatus could both sing, their English skills were quite limited, to say the least. They could've had nice careers in Europe, but that probably would've been the extent unless they mastered English. Neither singer had time for that, so their producer, Frank Farian, decided to do what he had done for some of his other musicians - have others actually sing the lyrics.

Farian had three men sing on Milli Vanilli's hit album, including American Charles Shaw, who did the rapping on "Girl You Know It's True."

But when you have a secret this big, it's bound to reveal itself eventually.

First, there was a mishap at a Milli Vanilli concert, when the recorded audio they were lip-syncing to skipped. That in itself wasn't that big of a deal, since many groups lip-sync at their live shows; but then Charles Shaw gave an interview in late 1989 stating that Morvan and Pilatus didn't sing on their album.

As all this was happening, Morvan and Pilatus wanted to prove their singing skills, so they started to pressure Farian to let them sing on the next album.

Farian had enough of it all by November 1990. He fired Morvan and Pilatus and revealed that they didn't sing a word of their chart-busting hits.

Milli Vanilli's epic failure behind the mic led to numerous personal and professional failures for the duo and their record label. They were stripped of their Grammy, lawsuits were filed against their label, Arista Records, and refunds were given to thousands who bought their album.

The worst part is that Morvan and Pilatus' careers went down the tubes.

They tried to rebound with a 1993 album where they actually sang, but it was a dismal failure. They even made commercials that parodied themselves and the situation, yet that too proved to be only a temporary fix.

Pilatus descended into a life of crime and drug and alcohol abuse, dying of a drug overdose in Germany in 1998.

Morvan has fared better than his bandmate, working as a producer and studio musician in the years since the debacle. Yet no matter what he does, he'll never be able to shake the fact that he was one half of the most epic fail in American music history.

8

THERE REALLY WAS SOMETHING BEFORE FACEBOOK

For many of you reading this, social media, and in particular, Facebook, play a major role in your lives, whether you like to admit it or not. You update your status multiple times throughout the day, are reliant upon it for news, and use it to stay abreast of happenings in your family such as marriages, births, and deaths.

It's hard to imagine life before Facebook.

But if you're under the age of 40, you remember life before Facebook, and you may also remember a social media website that was quite similar to it - Myspace.

Yes, way back in a calmer, gentler time - the mid-2000s - Myspace was the place to go for updates on news and your social network. More than 100 million people used Myspace in 2008, and it seemed to have no real competition.

But a year later, everything had changed, with Facebook becoming *the* social network and Myspace being relegated to just another epic fail in American tech history.

Myspace began its epic saga from the heights of the tech world to the depths of failure in 2003, when some tech nerds at a startup company eUniverse decided to rip off another early social networking site called Friendster (yes, even before Myspace there were still other social networking sites). The idea was simple: create a user-friendly website where anyone can have his or her own page to connect with friends, strangers, and just about anyone, anywhere.

The idea proved to be so successful that in 2005, Myspace was at the top of the social media world, but that also was the year when the company made its first and perhaps costliest mistake.

Mark Zuckerberg, who you probably know from Facebook fame, approached Myspace CEO Chad DeWolfe with an offer to buy his struggling, upstart social media site for $75 million.

DeWolfe held out for a better offer, which made him immensely wealthier but relegated his company to obscurity and the files of epic American failure.

DeWolfe sold Myspace to News Corporation (the company that owns Fox, Sky News, and other primarily film and television media companies) for a cool $580 million. By 2006, it seemed like a great deal for DeWolfe and Myspace, as the social networking site was registering 200,000 new users per day, but there were signs that they should've taken Zuckerberg's deal.

Facebook continued to exist in Myspace's shadow, slowly but surely gaining more and more users, especially college student millennials. Myspace's executives took a myopic view of Facebook and the social media market in general, preferring to look at the bottom line instead of emerging trends in media and technology.

And for a while, this was a good strategy.

In 2007, Myspace was valued at $12 billion, but the company's time at the top wouldn't last long.

When DeWolfe sold to News Corporation, it took him and the original company away from its roots and gave control of it to people who really didn't understand the internet. The boomers who bought Myspace tried to run it like it was Fox News or Sky News, with profits being the bottom line.

While that was going on, Zuckerberg was building his brand to the point that Facebook first overtook Myspace in the Alexa rankings in April 2008. But Zuckerberg continued to press the advantage by wooing existing Myspace users and enticing new social media users with a combination of slick marketing and user-friendly features. Facebook held the college crowd but was also able to draw older users because it was much easier to use and had a better reputation than Myspace.

In the years since Facebook overtook Myspace in 2008, Myspace has been through several changes of ownership but still continues to exist in a lonely part of the internet that relatively few people visit.

Myspace was a success for a while, but due to the shortsightedness of its founders, it failed to hold its spot at the top of the social media world.

9

NOT TOO BIG TO FAIL

Around the time Myspace began to fail in the social media world, the entire US economy began failing. Actually, the global economy began failing, which led to the economic recession of the late 2000s and early 2010s. As with any economic recession, there wasn't one single issue that was the cause, but among the reasons was the dominating power that many large Wall Street firms had on the economy.

These firms, such as Goldman Sachs and Merrill, don't really produce anything and are just in the money of making more money whichever way possible, from investing in real estate to trading in securities. Because these firms are so large in terms of money and comprise such a large part of the economy, American political leaders of both major parties deemed them "too big to fail" and used the taxpayer's money to bail them out of bankruptcy during the 2008 economic crisis.

But unfortunately for Lehman Brothers Holding Inc., since they were one of the first investment firms to have problems in the 2008 crisis, they were actually allowed to go into bankruptcy in what is probably America's largest economic fail.

The Lehman Brothers firm began before the Civil War with Henry and Emanuel Lehman, German-Jewish immigrants who started a small supply store in Alabama. They eventually got into the cotton and slave trade and made a fortune, before making even more money during the Civil War.

After the war, the Lehman brothers had built a dynasty that was based in New York City and had its hand in just about any kind of investing you could think of, from real estate to stock and bonds, and from precious metals to currency speculation.

By the middle of the 20th century, Lehman Brothers were *the* financial investment company, not just for Wall Street, but also for regular folks on main street who wanted to invest a little - or all - of their retirement savings.

And that's exactly why the Lehman Brothers were such an epic economic fail.

As more and more money from Middle America entered the Lehman Brothers' accounts, they began playing with their clients' money in riskier ways. Perhaps the biggest risk the firm took was handing out so-called subprime home loans, which often ended in default and contributed to the overall housing bubble of 2007-2008.

But Lehman Brothers also invested in risky stocks and unethical practices whereby it invested money it didn't have.

Then there was the management.

Lehman Brothers' top executives were known for their excessive salaries and greed, not to mention their general incompetence.

By the second quarter of 2008, the writing was on the wall, as Lehman Brothers recorded an astonishing $2.8 billion loss, sending its shares on the stock market down 45%.

It was all too much for the beleaguered and corrupt firm, which declared Chapter 11 bankruptcy on September 15, 2008.

Lehman Brothers' failure was felt immediately around the country.

It proved to be the largest bankruptcy in US history and immediately cost more than 26,000 people their jobs. The ripple effects were worse, though.

The US economy went into a downward spiral; millions of people lost their homes, jobs, and 401Ks; and the recession in America quickly spread to the rest of the world. The Lehman Brothers failure was the worst economic failure in a generation and is comparable to some of the worst economic failures in US history. One can only hope that the country's economic and political leaders learned something from the Lehman Brothers failure, but chances are, that'd be wishful thinking.

10

DID MONDALE EVEN
HAVE A CHANCE?

In terms of politics and government, there has been plenty of epic fails in the US. We've already looked at Pennsylvania politician Bud Dwyer's epic failure of a career that culminated in his very public suicide, so now let's take a look at Walter Mondale's failed 1984 presidential campaign.

Some of you reading this weren't around in 1984, so let's first go back a bit and look at the background and the two major candidates of that election.

Republican Ronald Reagan (1911-2004) was finishing his first term as the nation's 40th president in 1984, having faced some pretty stressful moments in those first four years. He inherited an economy that was plagued by inflation, had to contend with a Congress that was controlled by the Democrat Party and had to deal with the Soviet Union in a number of incidents in 1983 that threatened to turn the Cold War hot.

Not to mention, he'd survived an assassin's bullet in his third month in office!

But by 1984 the economy was doing well, and the Soviet threat had receded a bit, so Reagan's popularity was quite high.

The Democrat's nominated former Minnesota senator and vice president under Jimmy Carter, Walter Mondale (1928-2021).

You have to feel sorry a bit for Mondale, even if you're a Republican or someone who generally can't stand politicians.

Mondale was every bit the polite, mild-mannered Minnesotan, and he faced the unenviable task of trying to replace a popular, sitting president. He ran on what was at the time a liberal platform of anti-nuclear weapons, pro-tax, and pro-Equal Rights Amendment.

After both sides campaigned during the late summer and early fall, they met for two debates in October, where Mondale acquitted himself well, although the slight advantage probably went to Reagan.

But by that time, the vast majority of people had already made up their minds.

You have to realize that the United States was a lot less divided, more culturally homogenous, and more politically conservative in 1984. People didn't think in terms of "blue states" and "red states," and were often willing to cross party lines to vote for who they believed was the best candidate. And in 1984, it wasn't even close.

When Americans went to the polls on November 6 (early voting was only done under special circumstances back then), they overwhelmingly voted to give Reagan another term in one of the biggest election landslides in American history.

Reagan won 49 of the 50 states for a total of 525 electoral votes to just 13 for Mondale. Mondale did win his home state of Minnesota and the ultra-Democrat District of Columbia's three electoral votes, but he couldn't even win Democrat strongholds such as Massachusetts, Vermont, and Hawaii. It proved to be the most one-sided victory in terms of electoral votes since President Franklin Roosevelt defeated the forgettable Alf Landon in the 1936 presidential election.

Reagan also decimated Mondale in the popular vote. Reagan won 17 million more votes than Mondale, which was the second-largest margin of victory after President Richard Nixon's victory over the often-forgotten George McGovern in 1972.

Walter Mondale's 1984 presidential campaign is truly one of American politics' biggest fails, but in many ways, Mondale was set up to fail. He had the unfortunate - and one could argue, impossible - the task of trying to unseat one of the most popular presidents in history. Barring a major turn of events, Walter Mondale was doomed to fail, and fail big, in his 1984 presidential run.

The failure was so big that Mondale never ran for office again and for the most part, retreated from the public eye until his death.

11

THEY ACTUALLY THOUGHT
THEY COULD THROW THE
WORLD SERIES

What do you get when you mix personalities with the names Arnold "the Brain" Rothstein, "Shoeless" Joe Jackson, Chick Ghandil, and Kennesaw Mountain Landis with the 1919 Major League World Series?

The biggest fail in Major League Baseball's history.

Although nothing may be more American than baseball and apple pie, the sport of baseball has had its shares of ups and downs. When the National and American leagues came together to form Major League Baseball in 1903, it brought the best baseball players together in the world (this was before baseball was the international sport it is today) in one league. The players were professional, but there were no unions, free agency was still decades away, and the owners of the teams were known to take advantage of their players.

The situation was ripe for organized crime to move in.

By 1919, organized crime had made great inroads in the United States, especially in the world of sports betting. And when it came to sports betting, there was no gangster more capable, and feared, than Arnold "the Brain" Rothstein.

Rothstein was a Jewish gangster from New York City who favored using money and numbers rather than bullets and bats, but if he needed to, he could call on plenty of muscle, which included the likes of Charles "Lucky" Luciano and Meyer Lansky.

Rothstein liked to gamble, but he also liked to hedge his bets when he could by "fixing" boxing matches, horse races, or whatever sports event he could.

In 1919, disaffected members of the Chicago White Sox approached him with one of the biggest fixes in sports history that became one of America's greatest sports fails.

The fix began when a faction of the White Sox players, who later became known as the "Black Sox," led by Chic Gandil, decided they were going to stick it to owner Charles Comiskey and make some extra money in the process.

Gandil organized a meeting of like-minded players at a New York hotel room where they decided to go ahead with their plan. Although Rothstein himself never met with any of the players - he was a shrewd businessman and criminal - it's alleged he sent representatives to meet with some or all of the Black Sox faction. Once enough players agreed to the fix, it was just a matter of going through with it.

It would be a lucrative fix for all involved. Ringleader Gandil was paid $35,000 by the illegal bookies, while the other players involved got $5,000 each.

Not bad for 1917!

The problem was, though, that it was a best-of-nine game series, and the White Sox were heavy favorites. It would be hard making it look legit, and it soon became obvious to everyone watching that something wasn't quite right.

In game one, Sox pitcher Eddie Cicotte hit the batter on the second pitch of the game, which was a signal to all the conspirators, as well as those betting, that the fix was in. Sox pitcher Claude "Lefty" Williams did his part by losing a record three games in a World Series, but it made things look too obvious.

So, some of the Sox players decided to even things out a bit by winning games six and seven, although many experts argue that it was part of a double-cross that ended when the players were threatened by mafia thugs.

After the series ended, the victorious Cincinnati Reds returned home, the Black Sox and Arnold Rothstein took their pay, and everyone hoped to forget about it.

But things like this are just too big to file away, even in the era before TV and the internet.

Rumors began flying and during the middle of the 1920 baseball season, Cicotte confessed and implicated some of his teammates in the fix. Cicotte and seven of his teammates, including Shoeless Joe Jackson - who wasn't even at the meeting and whose involvement in the conspiracy has been questioned by later scholars - were indicted for conspiracy to defraud by the Cook County, Illinois district attorney in October 1920.

The eight men went to trial in the summer of 1921, with all being acquitted on July 28, 1921.

Many people around the country thought the fix was in again, including the Major League team owners.

The final chapter in this story of epic sports fail involves a character with a name as colorful as any of the players, Kennesaw Mountain Landis (yes, that was actually his name, which he got after his dad was wounded fighting for the Union at the Battle of Kennesaw Mountain in the Civil War).

Landis was a former federal judge, a baseball fan, and a no-nonsense straight shooter. The owners hired him as Major League Baseball's first commissioner, giving him considerable power to deal with the scandal. For Landis, the most reasonable act was to hand down a lifetime ban to all eight of the indicted players. They may have escaped criminal prosecution, but Landis believed they deserved to be held accountable for the rest of their lives.

The Black Sox scandal was such a great sports failure that many people believed it even had supernatural ramifications. After the scandal, the White Sox went on to be a perennial cellar dweller, only occasionally having competitive teams, leading many superstitious baseball fans (well, that's a bit of a redundant phrasing!) to believe the southside Chicago team was cursed.

Maybe they were. The White Sox epic 1919 World Series failure stayed with them until they finally won the series again in 2005, but for those eight players, it would be with them for eternity.

12

WAS IT AHEAD OF ITS TIME OR JUST DOOMED TO FAIL?

In many ways, American John DeLorean was an American success story. The son of European immigrants and a World War II veteran, DeLorean worked hard to become a successful engineer in the automotive industry. He was responsible for designing some popular and iconic American car models, such as the Pontiac GTO and the Chevrolet Nova. And as he designed cars, DeLorean worked his way upwards in General Motor's corporate ladder, proving that he was also a successful businessman.

But in other ways, DeLorean was an American failure story.

In 1975, thinking that he'd learned enough about engineering and business, DeLorean left GM and started his own automotive company, DeLorean Motor Company. After securing millions in loans and deals with the British government, DeLorean built a factory in Northern Ireland in 1978, but production delays meant that the first car wasn't sold until January 21, 1981.

DeLorean hyped his new car, called the DMC DeLorean, in a media blitz and at first, it looked like the futuristic-looking car was something made for the '80s.

Its gull-wing doors, silver-chrome color, and tinted, power windows were all features that made it a car of the future.

But from a business perspective, there were some real problems.

At $25,000 per car, most people couldn't afford to buy a DeLorean, and for those who could, it didn't compare favorably to other two-door sports cars. The DeLorean had a relatively weak six-cylinder engine and could only accelerate from 0-60 mph in 10.5 seconds. Those with money who wanted real power options could buy a Corvette.

By late 1981, DeLorean had only sold about 3,000 of the more than 7,000 cars produced. This was due to a number of reasons. First, once the novelty wore off, as mentioned earlier, true sports car enthusiasts with money could buy a Corvette, Porsche, or if they had a little more money, an Italian car, which all performed better.

Then there was the issue of dealers.

Most car manufacturers have affiliated car dealerships, but since DeLorean was an upstart company, it didn't have many.

Finally, the biggest problem was timing. When DeLorean released his futuristic car, it just so happened to be in the middle of a crippling recession and inflationary cycle. Most people who did have the money to spend were more interested in buying real estate and things other than cars.

DeLorean tried to get more funding for his company in 1982, approaching the British government and numerous private investors, but there were no takers.

DeLorean's final fall was when John was arrested for trying to buy $24 million of cocaine, which the government said he intended to sell to keep his company afloat. Although DeLorean beat the charges, he was forced into bankruptcy, forever relegating his futuristic car into obscurity.

Interest in the DMC DeLorean was revived when the 1985 blockbuster film *Back to the Future* featured one as a time machine. By then, however, it was a tongue-in-cheek cultural reference to something that may have been a great idea but for several reasons, was an epic failure.

13

THE GREAT CHICAGO FIRE AND FAIL

On October 8, 1871, Chicago, Illinois was a very different-looking city than it is today. It was obviously much smaller, with the area known today as the Near North Side being semi-rural and home to immigrants from Ireland, Germany, Poland, Italy, and various other European countries compared to today's predominantly white gentrification or the mainly African Americans just before them. It was in the Chicago city limits, but barns and farm animals were still common.

It was also the scene of one of the greatest fires, and fails, in American history - the Great Chicago Fire.

By the time the fire was completely extinguished on October 10, it had left a wake of destruction four miles long and ¾ mile wide, for a total of more than 2,000 acres. It destroyed 73 miles of streets and roads in Chicago, left more than 100,000 homeless, and most tragically, killed more than 300 people.

Several factors combined to allow the fire to happen, and then a series of human failures conspired to make it a tragedy.

It all started October 8 at the O'Leary home at 137 DeKoven Street. The legend goes that Mrs. Catherine O'Leary was milking a cow when the testy bovine kicked over a lamp or lantern, which sent the barn up in flames and then spread to the rest of the neighborhood. Although the O'Leary family would later deny the claim, the evidence shows that it did start at their residence.

Another theory posits that the fire began in the barn by gamblers who knocked over a lamp in a rush to avoid an angry Mrs. O'Leary, while yet another person states that a milk thief started the fire when he tried to avoid getting caught.

However, the fire, once it got going, it was fed by a combination of dry weather and a series of human failures.

The summer of 1871 was unseasonably hot and dry, which continued into the early fall. The conditions were perfect for a fire to start and spread, but it was other, human, failures that made things much worse.

First, the city of Chicago didn't have a proper water pumping system that could handle its growth. Although Chicago did have a modern waterworks system, it didn't serve all the residents. The people in the O'Leary family's neighborhood were unable to pump enough water to put the fire out themselves.

Also, somewhat ironically, the fire destroyed the city's waterworks anyway, which made pumping water to affected areas impossible.

Another failure was the type of construction used to build most of the homes in the burned areas. The construction industry boomed in cities such as Chicago after the Civil War.

To compensate for the immigrants filling up the cities, many contractors built homes quickly with cheap, wooden frames. The frames were flammable enough, but even more so was the tar used for the shingles on the roofs.

The houses went up like matches and the tarred roofs spat flaming embers hundreds of feet, further spreading the fire.

The O'Leary family sent word to the Chicago Fire Department almost immediately, and although the capable and relatively well-equipped department responded to the report promptly, they initially went to the wrong address!

Once the firefighters got to work, they couldn't stop the fire's spread, as it engulfed warehouse after warehouse that was storing coal, lumber, and other flammable materials. It also didn't help that in the era long before the Environmental Protection Agency, people and businesses regularly dumped flammable chemicals into the Chicago River.

The polluted river was unable to slow the fire.

By the late-night hours of October 9, the fire had begun to burn itself out and rain that evening helped to put out the last embers by the early morning hours of October 10.

After the damage of the Chicago Fire was finally assessed, the city's leaders realized that it was the result of a bizarre fail at the O'Leary residence, but was further spread by a series of human mishaps and failures that could've been prevented.

14

I BET YOU DIDN'T KNOW
LETTERMAN STARTED OUT
IN THE MORNINGS?

From February 1, 1982, until May 20, 2015, David Letterman was at the top of the late-night television genre. Until Johnny Carson retired in 1992, Letterman was consistently number two, but after Carson's retirement, he battled Jay Leno for the top spot.

Letterman's acerbic interview style, self-deprecating humor, sharp Midwestern wit, and guests that seemed to hit all the right notes worked wonders for the comedian. David Letterman seemed to instinctively understand the pulse of American pop culture in the 1980s, '90s, and 2000s like no other, but it almost never came to be.

As Letterman worked the comedy clubs in Los Angeles as a performer and writer during the 1970s, he began to turn heads in the industry. His dry sense of humor was a relief from the zany antics of many of the counterculture comedians of the

'70s, and before too long, he was performing on big stages such as *The Tonight Show Starring Johnny Carson*.

Executives at the NBC network were so impressed with Letterman's performances on Carson that they offered Letterman his own daily show, *The David Letterman Show*.

The former weatherman from Indiana was ecstatic about the offer; he would gain national exposure and make more money than he ever dreamed. There was one small problem, though - it was a daytime show.

NBC executives envisioned *The David Letterman Show* to be much like what *Late Night with David Letterman* later was, a modern era comedy and variety show. The two major differences were that the show was 90 minutes, and it was on in the mornings.

The David Letterman Show went on the air on June 23, 1980, with plenty of fanfare and support from the network, but it was immediately clear that it was a rating disaster. The show faltered until it was canceled just four months later on October 24, 1980.

And none of that was really Dave's fault.

Letterman told many of the same jokes, interviewed some of the same guests, did the same skits, and employed many of the same writers that he did two years later when he began his epic run in 1982. The failure of Letterman's daytime show was the fault of the NBC executives who put him on days.

NBC loved Letterman and knew they had a money-maker on their hands, but they thought he would help them win the daytime ratings against the other networks by bringing something new to the table with his sarcastic and sometimes edgy humor. But if you know anything about American TV habits in 1980, then you know he was clearly out of place.

Letterman was put in a slot where he competed against game shows and soap operas, both of which were the most popular daytime TV genres of the era. Letterman's growing fan base at the time was college students and people in their twenties, who were either in school, working, or sleeping when his show was on (this was long before DVR and most people still didn't have VCRs in the 1980s, especially broke college kids).

As epic a failure as *The David Letterman Show* was in many ways, Letterman was able to move past it, making it an often-overlooked chapter in a long and brilliant career.

15

AN EPIC FAILURE
IN BIRTH CONTROL

You may not know this, but birth control has been around since the dawn of civilization, and probably earlier. There are numerous birth control prescriptions from ancient Egypt, thousands of years old, many of which some quite dubious in their potential efficacy. For instance, I don't think crocodile dung had any true contraceptive qualities other than keeping men away from the woman who used it!

With that said, other home remedies, such as honey, may have had spermicidal qualities, and there were probably others from different cultures that have been lost. And when those didn't work, there was always the "rhythm method."

But most methods of birth control as we know it today are fairly modern inventions.

In the early 1900s, intrauterine devices (IUDs) were invented and hit the market for women who wanted more control over family planning. When the birth control pill hit the market in the 1960s, women were initially reluctant to use it, instead falling back on tried-and-true birth control methods such as intrauterine devices.

When the A.H. Robins Company purchased the Dalkon Corporation in 1970, they hoped to make a fortune off Dalkon's IUD, the Dalkon Shield. A.H. Robins executives believed it would be a win-win situation, where they'd make plenty of money and women would have increased access to safe birth control.

Except the Dalkon Shield proved to be quite unsafe and it destroyed the A.H. Robins Company, making it one of the biggest healthcare fails in American history.

The Dalkon Shield hit the market in 1971, about one year after A.H. Robins Company acquired it, and it immediately sold well. Robins marketed the Dalkon Shield as a safe alternative to the birth control pill, which was still somewhat of a wild card in the mid-1970s. More than three million women used the Dalkon Shield, but as more women used the IUD, many reported health problems.

Many women reported pains, some claimed the Dalkon Shield made them infertile, and in some cases, the fetus died from an infection known as septic abortion.

In the most extreme cases, the pregnant mother died.

In 1973, the Center for Disease Control (CDC) surveyed more than 35,000 obstetricians and gynecologists whose patients were using the Dalkon Shield, finding that more than 3,500 reported some adverse health effects. In 1975, the CDC published a lengthy report that showed the Dalkon Shield was unsafe and the cause of numerous, long-term health problems in many of the women who used it.

Further investigation revealed that the Dalkon Shield's design was faulty, as the string attached to the device that is used to remove it from the patient was made of multifilament string. This type of string is susceptible to the type of bacteria that can cause septic abortion.

A.H. Robins took the Dalkon Shield off the market in 1975, but the damage had been done. Individuals began filing lawsuits against the pharmaceutical company in the late '70s until there were 300,000 total, the largest such lawsuit since asbestos and the largest at the time against a drug company.

It was too much for A.H. Robins, which filed for Chapter 11 bankruptcy in 1985, making it one of the largest pharmaceutical failures in American history.

16

THE "PROFESSIONAL" HIT
ON NANCY KERRIGAN

The modern American media tends to glorify criminals. From the cool guys on *The Sopranos* to daring heist films like *Heat* and *The Getaway*, there's no shortage of anti-hero criminals in American television and film. And the ratings and box office numbers of these films and TV shows show that Americans really do love this stuff.

Most of us leave the glorified criminal world when we turn off our TV sets, but on January 6, 1994, a conspiracy of fools attempted to put a daring yet silly criminal plot into action, resulting in failure and prison time for most of those involved.

If you remember 1994, then chances are you may know what I'm talking about - the attack on American figure skater Nancy Kerrigan at the Cobo Arena in Detroit, Michigan. With that said, although the case grabbed headlines for a couple of months, it also disappeared just as quickly.

So, here's a recap of this epic sports and crime fail.

On the afternoon in question, Kerrigan was leaving the ice after practicing for the figure skating U.S. Championships, which was to determine the team for the 1994 Olympics. As she was walking down the hallway back to her dressing room, a man dressed in black emerged from behind a curtain and struck her in the leg with a telescopic baton similar to what the police use.

The man ran out of the arena into a waiting car and Kerrigan was left on the ground crying, "Why? Why? Why?"

The event was as bizarre as anything that's ever happened in American sports. Almost no one had a reason to attack Kerrigan, never mind do it in such a public way, so the police were at first baffled.

But once the FBI got involved, things started to turn toward her rival, Tanya Harding.

Harding, who was 23 at the time, was a working-class girl from Oregon who relied on sheer athleticism and strength in her routine. On the other hand, 24-year-old Kerrigan, who came from a middle-class New England family, dominated with grace and elegance.

Kerrigan won bronze in the 1992 Winter Olympics, so she was the odds-on favorite to lead the American team and was also a gold medal favorite.

Whether Harding couldn't deal with being second fiddle to Kerrigan or if her ex-husband Jeff Gillooly wanted to ride Harding's coattails to fame will probably never be known for sure, but once the FBI got involved, suspicion fell squarely on Harding.

The FBI focused on Gillooly, Harding's bodyguard Shawn Eckardt, Derrick Smith, and Shane Stant.

Under virtually no pressure, Eckardt confessed to the conspiracy and snitched on the other three, leading to their arrests.

Once the details of what these guys did emerged, then it was laughable. Gillooly was essentially the ringleader, paying Eckardt $6,500 to make it happen. Eckardt then subcontracted the "hit" (this motley crew of rejects actually referred to it as that term in recorded conversations) to his friend Derrick Smith, who then hired Shane Stant, the man who ultimately carried out the attack.

None of these guys was very bright, they had no military or police background, and none were seasoned criminals. Yet they all thought they were some sort of combination of Tony Soprano and Jack Bauer. Gillooly and company had fun live-action role-playing as "master criminals" and "special forces operatives," but when the going got tough, the crew turned on each other.

The farcical crew of criminals all received one- to two-year prison sentences and eventually faded into obscurity.

But what about Harding?

Harding continued to maintain her innocence and despite Gillooly giving a statement that implicated her in the entire affair, she continued to deny involvement until she went to the Olympics.

"Despite my mistakes and rough edges," Harding said at a press conference on January 27, 1994. "I have done nothing to violate the standards of excellence in sportsmanship that are expected in an Olympic athlete."

Harding had a bad performance at the Olympics, breaking a shoestring on one of her skates and finishing eighth overall, while Kerrigan won silver, which only added to the fact that the "hit" on Kerrigan was one of the biggest criminal fails in American history.

17

EVEL KNIEVEL'S EPIC FAIL

If you were a boy, young man, or adrenaline junky in the 1970s, there was no one cooler than Robert "Evel" Knievel. Knievel was a good ole' boy from Montana, who grew up with rodeos, hockey, skiing, and after he got a bit older, motorcycles.

Motorcycles became Knievel's true passion and by the mid-1960s, he made a name for himself in the western states as stuntman "Evel Knievel."

Evel's fame reached epic proportions when he attempted to jump the famous dancing water fountain at Caesar's Palace casino in Las Vegas, Nevada on New Year's Eve 1967. Although Evel cleared the fountain, he crashed on the other side and was hospitalized. But in the big scheme of things, it proved to be a success, as the jump was taped and later televised on ABC's *Wide World of Sports*, becoming the first of many appearances he made on the show.

Evel would go on to jump cars, buses, and trucks, usually successfully, but with some failures mixed in, although even the failures proved to be financially successful.

Knievel was also a savvy businessman. He built a definite brand around his image as an American hero wearing a red, white, and blue jumpsuit, risking his life by jumping into the unknown like the pioneers of the 19th century. He trademarked his name and image and sold it to be used for toys, movies, and TV shows in an era where that was quite rare. Truly, Evel Knievel was at the top of his game and was a part of American pop culture by the early '70s.

But then came his attempted jump at the Snake River Canyon.

By 1974, Evel Knievel had a sizable fan base and he had been putting the idea out there occasionally that he was going to attempt a jump of the Grand Canyon. Knievel knew, though, that a jump of the Grand Canyon was out of the question for legal and practical reasons, so he set his sights on the Snake River Canyon in southcentral Idaho.

At 500 feet deep and more than a quarter of a mile wide in parts, the Snake River Canyon seemed like a formidable yet doable jump for Knievel. Of course, he wouldn't be able to make the jump in a conventional motorcycle, so he had a steam-powered rocket named the Skycycle X-2 designed and built by engineer Doug Malewicki.

The failure began when Knievel couldn't come to an agreement with *Wide World of Sports* over payment, so the stuntman decided to hire a promoter to put the event on close circuit television to be shown on live TV at movie theaters.

Tickets to see the event live were $25.

Knievel launched across the canyon on September 8, 1974, at 3:30 p.m. local time, but as soon as he lifted off, the parachute prematurely deployed, which kept him from landing on the other side. Although he did make it the distance, the wind pushed the rocket back to the bottom of the other side of the canyon.

The fact that Evel failed that jump wasn't the worst part: he had failed previous jumps. No, what made the Snake River Canyon jump such an epic failure was the combination of the hype before the jump and all the money that private investors lost. The most notable loser in the investment was future professional wrestling mogul, Vince McMahon, who due to the loss, among other business failures at the time, was forced to declare bankruptcy in 1976.

For Evel Knievel, the failed jump at the Snake River Canyon marked the beginning of the end of his career as a daredevil. He would perform until the late 1970s, but he was a shadow of his former self.

18

YOU CALL IT A TELEPHONE?
I THINK WE'LL PASS

We all love our smartphones, but they wouldn't have been possible without landline phones. Some of us remember those days, when we actually had to remember people's phone numbers (and our own!), and when we had to find a payphone if we were away from home and wanted to make a call. That was pretty much the norm for decades.

When Alexander Graham Bell's telephone invention was granted a US patent in 1876, it revolutionized communication. By the end of that century, phones were common in major cities and by the 1920s, they were everywhere.

But how was long-distance communication conducted before the invention of the phone?

Various forms of signaling were used throughout history before the electrical telegraph was invented in the early 1800s. It was a system that could send messages as codes over hundreds of miles and almost instantly via cables that looked like telephone lines.

When the telegraph came to the United States, Western Union was *the* telegraph and communication company in the country.

In 1876, Western Union was one of the most successful companies in America and Alexander Bell was a young and successful inventor who was looking to become a successful businessman.

Bell knew that the patents to his technology were worth quite a bit of money, more than the $100,000 he offered to Western Union president William Orton. It was a lot of money, especially for 1876, and it proved to be more than Orton was willing to pay for the rights to the telephone.

For Orton, whose company essentially controlled communication technology in the era, there was no need for him to invest in new communication technology - or so he thought.

Of course, I don't need to tell you what a monumental failure Orton's refusal to buy Bell out was, but I will.

You only have to say the names "Orton" and "Bell" next to each other to know which one was more successful and had a bigger legacy. Orton's company did continue and found a niche with telegrams and bank wire transfers, but Bell proved to be the true visionary in science and business.

It's really funny how things work out. If Orton hadn't failed so miserably in this non-business deal, the world may have remembered his name, not Bell's.

19

WHEN THE CURE IS WORSE THAN THE DISEASE: ELIXIR SULFANILAMIDE

So far, the failures we've covered in this book have been pretty bad, but they didn't cost the lives of too many people. Of course, Bud Dwyer took his life and there were probably more than a couple of suicides due to the Lehman Brothers failure. The most tragic failure in terms of loss of life was the Chicago Fire, but the failure of Elixir sulfanilamide in 1937 comes close.

The early 1900s was a time of great change in America and the world. The emergence of the telephone, the invention of the radio, and the affordability of the Model-T automobile all made the world and country just a little smaller.

Great advances were also being made in medical science, with the development of antibiotic medicine in the early 1900s. The development, though, proved to be a mixed blessing and eventually resulted in one of the greatest failures in American medical history.

There's no doubt that the discovery of antibiotic medicine saved the lives of millions of people around the world and improved the health of millions more. As antibiotic medicine hit American shelves in the early 1900s, pharmaceutical companies, chemists, and even local pharmacists were able to experiment freely with prescriptions.

You see, there were very few laws on the books regulating drugs and medicine in the early 1900s, and the Food and Drug Administration wasn't established until 1930, and even then, it had very little power. So, with the American prescription drug landscape essentially a Wild West, it's no wonder that a very tragic, epic fail took place.

It's the case of a drug that was probably more fatal than any diseases it professed to cure.

It all began when pharmaceutical company S.E. Massengill launched Elixir sulfanilamide. Sulfanilamide was a standard antibacterial drug at the time, but since marketing was very important, the word "elixir" was applied because at that time it denoted a life-giving concoction that had a secret ingredient.

Well, not quite secret. Elixirs were required by law to have ethanol as an ingredient. In case you're wondering - yes, ethanol is the active ingredient in antifreeze.

In Elixir sulfanilamide's case, the secret ingredient was diethylene glycol (DEG), which although in the same chemical family as ethylene glycol, was a different chemical. It was then mixed with some raspberry flavoring and marketed as a wonder drug.

Massengill chief chemist Harold Watkins added DEG as an excipient, which is meant to stabilize the active ingredients of a drug and aid absorption, but it proved to be a fatal mistake. The product went on the shelves in September 1937, and in just one month, several deaths had been reported. By the time the drug was finally pulled from the shelves in 1938, at least 100 people had died from it, although due to the nature of record-keeping at the time and people's tendency not to report such things as much, the number is probably much higher.

When the American Medical Association (AMA) learned of the failure, it began an investigation that was then taken up by the fairly new Food and Drug Administration (FDA). The FDA learned that Massengill already knew about the danger of the drug and had sent a telegram to doctors, pharmacies, and salesman requesting the return of the drugs.

Finally, the FDA insisted that Massengill send out a much firmer message, which amounted to a recall.

When the gravity of the failure finally began to take effect, Dr. Samuel Massengill, the owner of S.E. Massengill, was forced to make a statement. Needless to say, it wasn't very contrite.

"My chemists and I deeply regret the fatal results, but there was no error in the manufacture of the product," Massengill said. "We have been supplying a legitimate professional demand and not once could have foreseen the unlooked-for results. I do not feel that there was any responsibility on our part."

By refusing to accept any real responsibility, Massengill essentially threw Watkins under the bus. After all, if the failure wasn't Massengill's fault, then it must be the chemist's, right?

Well, Watkins couldn't live with the shame, so he killed himself, becoming his deadly concoction's final victim.

As epic of a failure as Elixir sulfanilamide proved to be, it led to much-needed regulations in the drug industry.

20

NOT SO EASY A
CAVEMAN CAN DO IT

Our next entry in this illustrious hall of shame of American losers comes from 2007. It was a year that wasn't particularly known for anything special. The economic recession began toward the end of the year, but as with most economic downturns, it wasn't immediately felt until months later.

It was a year before a presidential election and although the wars in Iraq and Afghanistan were raging, nothing bad was happening at home.

But nothing good was going on either, at least not in terms of television.

Every fall the TV networks announce new lineups, hoping to have the next *Dukes of Hazzard* or *Friends* that will bring them ratings, money, and prestige. The key is to come out with something new, fresh, and hip that'll appeal to a younger crowd but will still be friendly enough to draw older people and families.

ABC thought they had a winning formula when they first aired their sci-fi (sort of) comedy (many would say that was debatable) *Cavemen* on October 2, 2007. They thought the premise was original (it wasn't) and since the characters were based on GEICO insurance commercials, that the public would readily identify with them (they didn't).

In the end, *Cavemen* was the biggest bomb of the 2007-2008 TV season and is one of the biggest fails of American TV history, and the producers of the show should've seen it coming.

The fail known as *Cavemen* began when ABC producers thought it was a good idea to turn a silly yet popular series of commercials into a full-fledged TV series. In case you're wondering, *Cavemen* was based on the GEICO commercials that featured Neanderthals living in the modern world, doing mundane, modern things, often ending the commercials with the line: "So easy a caveman can do it."

Well, apparently turning a popular commercial into a TV series wasn't so easy a modern human could do it!

As strange as the premise of cavemen living in the modern world was, it wasn't entirely original, which should've been the first sign for the producers not to do it.

During the 1966-1967 TV season, CBS put out a similar fail of a TV show called *It's About Time*. The premise of that show involved two astronauts traveling back in time to the Prehistoric Age and then back to the 1960s with a family of cavemen who have to adjust to being outsiders in the modern world.

This failed concept was essentially the same as that of *Cavemen*.

The truth is, though, *Cavemen* didn't know what type of TV show it was. It appeared to be sci-fi but how Neanderthals/cavemen survived into the modern world was never explained, which would've been fine if it was done with some humor, but all the jokes seemed to fall flat.

And as bad as the jokes were, the direction of the writing was worse. In some episodes, *Cavemen* appeared to take a social commentary position, substituting different ethnic groups for the cavemen in the show, but it all seemed forced and derivative.

The network pushed the show hard with promo after promo, but it just wasn't enough to help it survive. Once people tuned in to watch *Cavemen*, they saw what an epic fail it was and tuned out. *Cavemen* was canceled midway through its first season and only six episodes were aired.

But as much of a TV fail as *Cavemen* was, it wasn't the biggest fail in American TV history. We'll get to that show a bit later.

21

WITH A NAME LIKE EDSEL, NO WONDER IT FAILED

Well, maybe the name wasn't so bad; it was, after all, the name of one of Henry Ford's sons, and if it was good enough for the founder of the Ford Motor Company, it should've been good enough for a name of a series of cars Ford rolled out from 1958 through 1960, right?

Wrong.

The name "Edsel" became synonymous with poor marketing, bad business practices, and overall strange design. However, many experts also cite the car's unique name as one of the reasons for its failure. The reality is that there were many problems associated with the Edsel line, all of which combined to make it the worst automotive failure in American history.

When the Ford Motor Company became a publicly traded company in 1956, the Ford family lost most of its influence on decision-making. Founder Henry Ford had been dead for almost ten years by that time and a new generation of entrepreneurs and engineers had taken over the company.

They had big plans to bring the company into the latter half of the 20th century, the first of which was the Edsel line of cars.

The first problem with this new line was the name. The Ford family wasn't crazy about using it, which perhaps was a sign of things to come, but the company moved ahead with production. Ford also developed a network of dealers to sell the new cars and invested heavily in a marketing campaign so that when they first rolled out in 1958, there would be people waiting to buy them from coast to coast.

Except that never happened.

Although sales in the first year weren't bad - more than 63,000 were sold in the US and nearly 5,000 in Canada - they were below expectations. Ford executives immediately began looking around for problems.

Perhaps there were too many models?

There were four sedans and two station wagon models of the Edsel on the market in 1958, so for 1959, that number was trimmed to two sedans, the Ranger and Corsair, and one station wagon, the Villager.

Yet sales dropped even more.

For 1960, Ford only produced the Ranger and the Villager and made many design changes, but it was too little too late. Ford admitted that the Edsel was a complete failure and discontinued the line in late 1959 but continued to produce 1960 models until the end of November 1959 (American car models are produced and begin being released toward the end of the previous year, for example, the 2021 model began being released in late 2020).

When the Edsel was officially declared dead, carmakers, engineers, and businessmen associated with the automotive industry all took a step back to see what went wrong.

And as they looked, they found plenty!

The most notable problem with the Edsel was its design. On the one hand, it really wasn't very original, using the body of other Ford-owned cars such as the Ford and Mercury. Because of this, customers didn't really know how it was so different from a Ford or a Mercury. However, the Edsel did have some small but very notable design features that set it apart - for the wrong reasons.

The most notable was its weird oval-shaped grille. It wasn't very popular with Americans, who thought it looked like a horse collar. In 1958, Americans were trying hard to leave their agrarian past in the past and didn't want to be reminded of it.

Then there were the rear taillights on the 1958 station wagons. They were boomerang-shaped, which was very 1950s, but they pointed inward instead of outward, which was confusing at night when the blinkers were used. For instance, if the driver used the right blinker to indicate a right turn, the right taillight actually seemed to point left.

The Edsel also had many dashboard features that were state-of-the-art and resembled controls on a plane more than a car at the time. Ford executives, though, believed the crowning achievement of the new controls would be the Teletouch transmission controls.

The Teletouch was simply a gear-shifting mechanism that instead of being utilized via a gear stick on the floor or the steering column, was done through buttons on the wheel. It was believed that customers would love the new feature and find it much easier to use. Instead, they found it confusing as they often shifted when they meant to use the horn.

Edsel's epic failure can also be attributed to poor marketing.

Besides the very uncool name, even by late '50s standards, the cars were poorly marketed. Ford executives and advertisers never gave the Edsel a personality and because they were made partially from Ford and Mercury designs, Americans really didn't know which one they were.

And the pricing didn't help either.

Edsels were priced in the same range as Mercuries, forcing the upstart line to compete with its well-established sister line. Why would loyal Ford-Mercury customers buy a goofy-looking Edsel when they could get a similarly priced, reliable Mercury?

It wasn't happening.

And another thing that wasn't happening was the global economy in 1958. When the Edsels first rolled out, the Recession of 1958 had been raging since August 1957 and would continue to do so until April 1958. Although the recession wasn't as bad as some previous and later recessions, it was enough to cut consumer spending.

Americans cut back on what they bought, and at the top of the list were high-end items such as cars. The cars that were sold during the Recession of 1958 were either lower-priced Fords or reliable, mid-priced Mercuries.

By 1959, no one wanted nor needed an Edsel.

Today, refurbished Edsels can fetch unusually high prices from interested collectors, but they stand as testaments to the absolute failure of an entire line of automobiles.

22

THE MOVIE THAT KILLED A GENRE, AND ALMOST CLOSED A STUDIO

On June 12, 1963, American film-goers finally got to see the much-hyped and critically acclaimed film *Cleopatra* starring Elizabeth Taylor in the title role, Richard Burton as Mark Anthony, and stage and film legend Rex Harrison as Julius Caesar. Other notable actors in the film included Rowdy McDowall as a young Octavian/Augustus, Carroll O'Connor as Servilius Casca, and Michael Hordern as Cicero.

In addition to its all-star cast of actors, *Cleopatra's* expensive sets were historically authentic, and its plot was also historically accurate, and well-written.

Filming took about two years to complete and when it was done, the version that was shown in the movie theaters was more than three hours long.

The length of the film wasn't out of the ordinary for its genre, the epic, which had become very popular by the early 1960s. *The Ten Commandments* and *Lawrence of Arabia* were two of the more popular films in the genre that came out before *Cleopatra*, but there were scores of others.

Many of the epics of the late 1950s and early '60s took place in medieval or ancient times, which led to the creation of a subgenre known as "sword-and-sandal" films. As the name infers, these films took place in the ancient world and usually involved plenty of violence. They were often low-budget and made in Italy but were usually quite popular and financially successful.

So, in 1959, the executives at Twentieth Century Fox Film Corporation decided to take advantage of the success of the epic and sword-and-sandal genres by making their own big-budget film. Twentieth Century spared no expenses in *Cleopatra* by hiring top director Joseph Mankiewicz and the best American and British actors that money could buy.

Twentieth Century Fox also didn't cut corners when it came to costumes or sets and filmed on location in Italy.

Long before the film was released, Fox executives realized it was costing them more than they could afford. Fox had to shut down production on other projects to pay for the ballooning budget of *Cleopatra*.

The final cost for the film was $44 million, which was astronomical in 1963.

Still, Fox had high hopes that ticket sales would help them go into the black.

Although *Cleopatra* was probably a bit too long for most people to sit through, it was far from a bomb. Global ticket sales were brisk, and critics loved everything about it, but it wasn't enough for Fox's bottom line.

In the end, Fox made just over $40 million from its share of the ticket sales, which put it in the red and in danger of going bankrupt. Fox was only saved by cutting back on the production of other films, selling one of its own studio lots, and selling the rights to *Cleopatra* to the ABC TV network for $5 million.

Although Twentieth Century Fox may have just barely survived, the epic and sword-and-sandal genres didn't fare quite as well.

Major American film studios all but killed the idea of the epic for decades thanks to Fox's experience with *Cleopatra*. A few were made here and there, but nowhere near the numbers of the late 1950s and early '60s, and today they are still fairly rare.

Italian filmmakers also ditched the sword-and-sandal genre by the mid-1960s in favor of the spaghetti Westerns.

23

AMERICA'S BIGGEST BANK FAILS

Good or bad, money is often at the core of anything big that happens. We've seen so far that many of these big fails were big fails due to money problems. If a product such as the USFL, *Cleopatra*, the DeLorean, or the E.T. video game doesn't make enough money, it's bound to be a failure.

And when it comes to the business of making money, this is especially true.

Earlier we looked at how the Lehman Brothers scandal brought down one of the biggest banking and investment firms in American history, but did you know that nearly 200 years earlier two major banks were brought down by politics?

The First Bank of the United States and later the Second Bank of the United States was established to bring economic and banking uniformity to the new nation in the late 1700s and early 1800s. As the country was still trying to find its legs in those early years, many believed that a strong central bank was needed that could serve the entire country.

Not everyone agreed.

As the debate raged about the idea of a national bank, the First Bank of the United States came to a rather inauspicious end, but in a few years, it was replaced. The Second Bank of the United States would also fail, although its demise was much more spectacular and left a bigger imprint on American history and culture.

After the United States became an independent country and the Constitution was signed delineating powers to the federal government and individual states, as well as the rights of the citizens, early leaders focused on how to keep the country united, safe, and strong.

The Federalist Party believed in using the central government to achieve those goals.

Among the Federalists was Alexander Hamilton, who served as first Secretary of Treasury. Hamilton was a pretty smart guy and a keen economic thinker. He believed that the new nation desperately needed a national, central bank, so he advocated for the First Bank of the United States.

Hamilton's proposal was accepted by Congress and signed into law by President Washington in 1791, but it was only given a 20-year charter.

The bank was never very popular with the largely agrarian American population, so in 1811 its charter was allowed to lapse.

No harm, no foul.

The idea kept circulating, though, for the next several years, even as the Federalist Party collapsed. Then in 1816, the Second

Bank of the United States was proposed with a 20-year charter. With the Democratic-Republicans in almost complete control of the government, it was easily passed by Congress and signed into law by President James Madison.

The Second Bank of the United States immediately proved to be quite divisive.

Although the First Bank of the United States was not a true central bank in the modern definition - it did not set monetary policy or act as a lender of last resort - it printed the national currency and had branches in every state.

As innocuous as this may sound, many thought it infringed on states' rights, while those who favored money backed by gold or silver thought its policy of fiat money was unsound.

When Andrew Jackson was elected president in 1828, things didn't immediately change, but by the end of his first term, they were quickly moving that way. Jackson was a Democrat, and in general, the Democrats and Democrat voters were distrustful of the Second Bank of the United States, to say the least.

The other major party at the time, the National Republicans, generally favored the Second Bank of the United States, so when Jackson began his "war" against the bank, it was partially due to politics.

When Jackson won re-election in 1832, he made dissolving the Second Bank of the United States his number one policy. He just couldn't wait until the bank's charter had expired, so he began removing the bank's deposits, with questionable means and legality, to private banks.

No matter: the banks were even less popular then than they are today, so most people didn't have a problem with what Jackson had done. The charter ran out in 1836 and after being a private bank for five years, the Second Bank of the United States was finally liquidated in 1841.

The failure of the First and Second Banks of the United States had long-lasting impacts on the country after they were gone. The economic Panic of 1837 is at least partially blamed on the collapse of the Second Bank, and the failure of the two banks, in general, is often cited as a reason why the United States didn't establish a national bank again until the Federal Reserve system in 1913.

24

NEVER MESS WITH SUCCESS

If you're eating a very American slice of apple pie and watching the very American sport of football, what's the most American drink you can think of to go with it?

Many of you probably thought Coca-Cola, right?

Not long after Coca-Cola hit the market in 1886, it became an American classic and popular throughout the nation. Some argue that the reason why it caught on so quickly is that small amounts of cocaine were used in the ingredients until 1904, while those less cynical say it was simply because of the taste and marketing. Whatever the reason, Coca-Cola, or "Coke" as it became known, was America's most popular soft drink for nearly 100 years.

But by the early 1980s, things began to change.

In the late 1970s, Pepsi-Cola embarked on a massive marketing campaign to unseat Coke as the top cola in America by hiring rock stars to promote their product in ads. Pepsi was portrayed as a hipper, newer drink for Americans, which was summed up with their slogan: "Pepsi, the choice of a new generation."

Another effective marketing ploy the executives at Pepsi thought up was bringing the "Pepsi Challenge" to middle America.

The Pepsi Challenge could be found at pretty much every mall in America. It was usually simply a booth where "blind" sample drinks of Pepsi and Coke were given to participants. You picked which one you thought tasted better and the person working the booth revealed your pick.

Pepsi usually won.

And by the mid-1980s, Pepsi was winning in supermarket sales, although Coke was holding on with vending machine and restaurant sales.

But for Coca-Cola, hanging on wasn't good enough. They had to be *the* cola drink in America, and the only way to reclaim that mantle was by doing something big. So, Coca-Cola CEO Roberto Goizueta decided that if you couldn't beat Pepsi, Coke would join them by changing its formula to a sweeter taste that was closer to Pepsi's. The new formula would also be rebranded as "New Coke," and most important, the original brand was to be eliminated.

New Coke was rolled out on April 23, 1985, with plenty of fanfare, and although it was initially popular, resentment toward the new brand quickly built.

Especially in the South.

Because Coca-Cola was born in Atlanta, Georgia and still has its headquarters there today, Southerners have traditionally looked at Coke as one of "their" products. If you've ever been to the Southern states, you know the people don't call carbonated soft drinks soda pop or pop, they refer to it all as "Coke," no matter the brand, flavor, or type. So as much as Coke may be a part of the American cultural fabric, it's even more so in the South.

But negative reactions to New Coke reverberated across the United States and beyond. Foreign Coke distributors weren't too keen on the new brand either, so by summer, it became clear that the experiment was a dismal failure.

Coca-Cola brought back its original formula on July 11, 1985, just 79 days after the failed experiment of New Coke got underway. New Coke continued to be sold alongside the original formula for a number of years and was itself rebranded as "Coke II," although it was never a big seller.

As big a failure as New Coke was, though, it did help bring Coke back into prominence, regaining its position as *the* American cola. Coca-Cola learned the valuable lesson that when you have a good thing going, don't mess it up!

25

BOTCHED SUICIDE OR BOTCHED ASSASSINATION?

When journalist Gary Webb was found dead in his Carmichael, California home on December 10, 2004, it immediately raised suspicions. Webb was famous for uncovering a drug trafficking plot by the Contra rebels in Nicaragua during the 1980s, which he argued was done under the watchful eyes of CIA agents. Once the cocaine was smuggled into the US, it was sold by American Ricky Ross to black gangs in south-central Los Angeles, who then turned it into crack.

The accusations were well-documented and published as a series called "Dark Alliance" in *The Mercury News* in 1995, which Webb later turned into a best-selling book, *Dark Alliance.*

Needless to say, the CIA denied that they were involved in any wide-scale drug trafficking operation and that although some of their Contra assets may have done so, they in no way condoned or knew what was happening.

Although Webb received support from some politicians, most in government, as well as his fellow journalists from *The New York Times* and *The Los Angeles Times*, said that many of his claims were baseless and were conspiracy theories.

Still, the idea that the CIA at least looked the other way while drugs were being smuggled into the US was at least plausible in most people's minds.

And when Gary Webb was found with two gunshot wounds to his head, it seemed to many, to be retribution for his expose.

Despite the circumstances, Sacramento County Coroner ruled the death a suicide and when asked how a person could kill himself with two shots to the head, his only answer was, "It's unusual in a suicide case to have two shots, but it has been done in the past, and it is a distinct possibility."

So, technically Webb could've killed himself, but with two shots it would've been a botched suicide. Many people just can't buy that and think there's no way Webb wasn't murdered. Even if the CIA or Contra assets didn't do it, you only have to look at Webb's career to see there was no shortage of people who had motives.

Webb began his journalism career in the late 1970s and early 1980s investigating political corruption and organized crime in Kentucky and Ohio. After exposing some pretty influential people, he moved to California where he focused on the CIA-Contra-black gang drug connections.

So, if Webb was assassinated, a number of different players could have been responsible. The reality is, though, that if Webb was murdered and the killers attempted to make it look like a suicide to throw investigators and the public off the trail, they failed miserably.

The double shot to Webb's head, combined with his investigative journalism background, made the death look very suspicious.

With that said, Webb's wife, Sue Bell, publicly stated that Webb was depressed about the course of his career and that she believes he did commit suicide. As the coroner noted, double headshot suicides are extremely rare but not impossible. After the first shot, the hand could've jerked and reflexively fired a second shot or Webb survived the first shot and then fired the second shot.

Whether it was a botched suicide or botched assassination, the death of Gary Webb is one of the most bizarre fails in American history.

26

FUGGETABOUTIT: MCDONALD'S FAILS AT GOING ITALIAN

As American as apple pie and Coca-Cola are, you have to admit that McDonald's is too. Sure, Mickey D's is greasy, unhealthy, and generally nasty, but it hits the spot when you're hungry. And it's convenient too. Just about any American city of 5,000 people or more has a McDonald's, so chances are, wherever you are in the US, if you have a hankering for some greasy fast food, the golden arches aren't too far away.

Yes, for better or for worse, McDonald's is a true American institution that serves the saltiest versions of American food, but Americans like more than just burgers and fries, right?

Italian food generally and pizza specifically are among the most popular foods in the US. No matter if you're from Brooklyn or Boise, Americans love spaghetti and fettuccine and although we may argue over New York thin slice or Chicago deep dish being the better style, most love pizza.

So, it would seem logical to take the American institution of McDonald's and combine it with America's love of Italian food, right? Well, it may have seemed logical in the late 1970s, but it proved to be an epic failure!

Beginning in the late 1970s, many McDonald's locations started offering "Italian" fare on their menus. Calling what they sold Italian is being very generous with the term, but they did sell versions of spaghetti, fettuccine, and even lasagna. Or at least, that's what they told us it was.

The items looked as bad as they tasted. For instance, the spaghetti consisted of a box of wormy-looking noodles served with a watery tomato paste, and what were apparently chunks of tomatoes.

Needless to say, the "Italian" items proved to be a bomb and were discontinued by McDonald's in most locations by the mid-1980s, but for some reason, the fast-food giant didn't get the point.

McDonald's decided once more to move far outside of its lane when it introduced personal pan pizzas in the late 1980s.

Do you remember that?

Don't feel bad if you don't, because they were only available at limited locations for a very limited time. And I mean *limited*!

The issue wasn't so much the quality of the pizzas, but more so that it took ten minutes to make one; they didn't have any waiting to go like many pizza places do today. Not only that, but who wanted to go to McDonald's for a pizza in 1989?

McDonald's may be the premier fast-food chain in America, and probably the world, and Americans truly love Italian food, but that doesn't mean those two things should ever be put together. McDonald's learned a hard lesson about consumer tastes in the 1980s when they failed to sell Italian at the golden arches.

The people took one look at that soupy spaghetti in a box and said "fuggetaboutit!"

27

THE AMERICAN PARTY, THE GREENBACKS, AND OTHER FAILED POLITICAL PARTIES

The American political system has been a two-party political system since its beginning. It's not written that way in the constitution, but a number of elements in the way the political system has developed have prevented it from becoming a multi-party system.

Perhaps the primary factor that has kept the US a two-party system is the "winner-takes-all" method of elections. Instead of awarding congressional seats proportionately by the percentage a party gains in an election, each congressional district is awarded to the sole winner of the race. The same is true with the Senate and the presidency, although the president is elected by the electoral, not the popular vote.

Third parties also often find it difficult to get enough signatures to make it onto the ballot in many states and in the modern era, TV debates have generally prohibited third-party candidates.

But that's not to say that third parties have always been a failure.

The Republican Party began as a third party just before the Civil War, and the Whig Party formed as a successful third-party challenge to Andrew Jackson and the Democrats in 1833, becoming the second major party until they were in turn replaced by the Republicans in 1856. Although the Whigs only lasted 20 years, they were far from a failure.

But there have been some very interesting, very short-lived third parties in American history that for one reason or another failed.

The first major third party in American politics was actually a one-issue party that was built on conspiracy theories - the Anti-Masonic Party. The Anti-Masonic Party formed in 1828 in New York after an outspoken former Freemason, William Morgan, disappeared. Morgan's disappearance was a sign to many that America was being taken over, or already had been, by nefarious members of the secret orders of the Freemasons. The Anti-Masons made it their mission to illuminate the inner workings of the Illuminati.

In many ways, the Anti-Masons were the Q-Anon of their day, except they ran candidates under their own party.

And the Anti-Masons had some pretty influential support, such as future president John Quincy Adams.

At the height of their influence, the Anti-Mason Party successfully won the governor's houses in Vermont and Pennsylvania and elected many members to state congressional houses and the US Congress in many northeastern states.

Still, as successful as the Anti-Masons were initially, their run was over by 1840. The idea of a one-issue party didn't appeal to most Americans, especially when it was something that most Americans had no experience with, as was the case with Freemasons. Once the Whig Party formed, it slowly but steadily took members from the Anti-Masons, eventually relegating it to an interesting footnote in American history.

The next major third-party fail began as a social movement but was later co-opted by the Republican Party.

In the 1850s, there's no doubt that slavery was the central issue of most political discussions, but running a close second was immigration. Large numbers of primarily Catholic immigrants from Ireland and Germany had flocked to cities in the northeast during the 1840s and '50s, causing some social tensions and anxiety for the generational Native American population.

The anxiety turned into anti-immigrant sentiment, which was organized at secret lodges and societies that became known as "Know Nothing" organizations because when asked about their involvement in such groups, the members would reply they "knew nothing."

Like the Anti-Masons before them, the Know-Nothings became popular in the Northeast and even mounted a bid for the presidency in 1856, as the American Party, with Millard Fillmore as their candidate.

Fillmore didn't do very well because by that point the American Party/Know-Nothings were all but done as a third party. The upstart Republican Party, which focused on stopping the spread of slavery, adopted some anti-immigrant rhetoric to draw Know Nothings into their party.

It worked because, by the time the Civil War started, no one in America could even remember the Know-Nothings.

The next American third party that failed is interesting because they were actually *for* inflation. The Greenback Party formed in 1874 to challenge many of the corporate monopolies that were forming at the time in the railroad and mining industries. The Greenbacks believed that the most effective way to help small business people and farmers and to challenge the monopolies was by printing money that *wasn't* backed by gold or silver.

The Greenbacks were able to win a few seats in Congress, and although some of the other issues they advocated resonated with members of both political parties, the Democrats and Republicans were quite opposed to them on principle.

When the United States became part of the informal "classical gold standard" in 1879 by paying its debts in gold, the Greenbacks' days were numbered. They continued to press the issue but by 1889, it was clear the US was staying with gold, so the Greenbacks dissolved.

The 20th century would witness a number of failed third parties.

There was the Progressive Party of 1912-1920, better known as the "Bull Moose Progressive Party," which was formed by former Republican President Theodore Roosevelt (1858-1919) after he lost the 1912 Republican presidential nomination.

Although Roosevelt was beaten by Democrat Woodrow Wilson (1856-1924), he placed second, possibly costing his former friend and Republican President William Taft (1857-1930) a second term.

But the Bull Moose Progressives were a party built on a personality, so when Roosevelt died, he took the party with him.

Some other failed third parties you may have heard about (or probably not), include the pro-segregation State's Rights Democratic Party of 1948 and George Wallace's American Independent Party of the 1968 presidential election. These parties failed when the institution of segregation was dismantled across the South.

There are plenty of third parties in the US today, such as the Libertarian Party, the Reform Party, and the Green Party, and although none of them has made a major breakthrough, we'll reserve judgment on calling them failures.

Give them a few more years, though, and if they still haven't done anything then you can add them to this list.

28

JARTS: THROWING DEADLY MISSILES AROUND WAS FUN FOR A MINUTE

What happens when you take the once-popular American backyard activity of horseshoes and mix it with an ancient Greek weapon?

You get Jarts, the game where people threw 12-inch-long missiles - javelins really, thus the portmanteau "jarts" - around their yards, sometimes with disastrous consequences. Lawn darts, as they were more generally known - Jarts was just the most popular brand of lawn darts - first came out in the 1950s, as more and more Americans moved to the suburbs and needed something to do with their time when they weren't working.

So, what better way to enjoy your new suburban backyard than throwing around small javelins, right?

Well, as crazy as the game sounds, the game play was pretty simple. Each set came with four or five jarts. Each jart has four plastic fins on a rod, and at the other end is an approximately four-inch weighted and slightly pointed tip. Yes, that's where the danger, and some would say fun, comes from.

Each set also came with two rings. The object was to divide into teams, space each ring about 35 feet from each other, and take turns attempting to throw your team's colored ring into your assigned ring. The rules varied, but if you were a kid growing up in the '70s or '80s, chances are you made up your own Jarts' rules.

Kids would throw them straight up in the air to see how far they would go, or they would throw them at trees, walls, or other objects that weren't meant to have jarts hurled at them.

And of course, some kids even threw them at each other from time to time.

Throughout the 1980s Jarts were responsible for more than 6,000 Americans making visits to the emergency room, but only one child, 7-year-old Michelle Snow, is known to have been killed by a jart.

After Michelle was killed by an errant jart in 1987, her father, David Snow, decided that he was going to do something about the jart scourge in America. Long before cancel culture was even a term in America, David Snow started a crusade to rid the world of the evil game known as Jarts.

But as silly as this may sound, Snow's campaign ultimately proved to be successful.

After appearing on talk shows and getting the ear of state and federal lawmakers, Snow's campaign against Jarts attained victory when the United States Consumer Product Safety Commission banned all lawn dart games in December 1988. The ban put an end to jarts' games around the country.

I guess not everyone thought Greek javelins and horseshoes were a good combination!

29

THE MINNESOTA VIKINGS AND BUFFALO BILLS: EPIC SUPERBOWL FAILURES

When you look at the history of the National Football League (NFL), the Minnesota Vikings and Buffalo Bills should stand out as two of the most successful franchises of all time. Both teams have amassed exceptional overall records, have had a number of Hall of Fame players, and boast of sizable and loyal fanbases for mid-sized media market teams.

But both the Vikes and Bills are epic Super Bowl failures.

When it comes to the NFL, nothing else really matters other than how many Super Bowl rings you have on your fingers. The records are nice, the fans are great, but unless you can claim to have won the biggest game in American football, you really can't claim to be the best.

For the Minnesota Vikings, their road to fame, and infamy, began when they became an expansion team in the National Football League in 1961, which later became the National Football Conference when the old NFL merged with the

American Football League (AFL) to form the current version of the NFL in 1970.

The first few years were tough, with the Vikes losing most of their games, but head coach Bud Grant was building a gritty team identity that would come to dominate what would become the NFC for about ten years beginning in the late 1960s. Known as the "Purple People Eaters," the Vikings' defense was led by Jim Marshall and Alan Page, who were known to be extra tough and to thrive in the cold outdoor stadium the Vikings played in at the time.

Hall of Fame quarterback Fran Tarkenton led the offense for most of their glory years, but in 1969, they were led by Joe Kapp. The 1969 Vikings were the heavy favorite going into Superbowl IV in New Orleans, but they bombed bigtime, losing to the Kansas City Chiefs 23-7.

But the Purple People Eaters would be back, and they had Tarkenton commanding the offense.

No matter, the Vikings lost Superbowl VIII and IX in consecutive years and then took a year off from losing Superbowls; only to come back and get blown out by the Oakland Raiders 32-14 in Superbowl XI.

As great an organization as the Minnesota Vikings were, they became somewhat of a laughing-stock; they were choke artists and the ultimate Superbowl failures at 0-4.

Vikings fans lamented their lowly, and lonely, position as the only 0-4 Superbowl team in the NFL, but then the 1990s came and the Vikings got a little company in the world of Superbowl fails.

The Buffalo Bills were one of the charter teams of the American Football League in 1960, and as one of the more successful AFL teams on and off the field, were incorporated into the NFL when the two leagues merged.

The Bills didn't have the same early success in the NFL that the Vikings did, but over time, they developed their own unique identity under head coach Marv Leavy. Like the Vikings, who although hundreds of miles away played at almost the same latitude, the Bills became a gritty team who used the cold and snow of their outdoor stadium to their advantage.

So, by the 1990s, the Buffalo Bills had some of the best players in the NFL. Led by hall of fame quarterback Jim Kelly, who often handed the ball to Thurman Thomas, or passed to Andre Reed, the Bills had become the dominant AFC team by 1990.

Then there was Super Bowl XXV. The game was close, but the Bills marched down the field in the closing seconds and were poised to win on a field goal. But Bills' kicker Scott Norwood missed the chip shot wide right, losing the game 20-19.

The Bills went on to lose the next three Superbowls, and like the Vikings, they would never get another chance in the big game.

Some people think Norwood's missed chip shot cursed the Bills, but the reality is, sometimes in sports, things just happen that way. The Buffalo Bills can only blame themselves for being epic Superbowl failures. You'd think that eventually either the Vikings or Bills will win a Superbowl, but if you're a fan of either team, you probably think that's asking a bit too much.

Since the Vikings and Bills are from different conferences, there's the chance that they could meet in a Superbowl and one of them would walk away with a win, right? Who knows, though, with the way these two teams have failed in Superbowls, a terrorist attack, the arrival of aliens, or some other type of catastrophic event would probably happen, and the game would be canceled.

30

DO YOU REMEMBER NAPSTER? PROBABLY NOT

When compact discs began replacing cassette tapes in the 1980s, everyone thought they were a miracle of music technology. CDs were a bit easier to store than tapes and their sound quality was much better. They also didn't get stuck in players the way tapes did.

But by the mid-1990s, it was apparent that CDs weren't the futuristic music media we all thought they'd be. They scratched easily and although they were a bit easier to store than tapes, they were still a bit bulky.

The mini-CD came out in the 1990s, but it never caught on, partially because the '90s was the beginning of the internet age and the start of a new era in music media.

By the late '90s, all the cool kids were downloading all their music onto their computers in MP3 format.

In those early years, most people simply recorded their CDs on their computers into MP3 format, but in 1999, techies Shawn

Fanning and Sean Parker came up with a way for music fans to download songs and albums directly from a website.

On June 1, 1999, Fanning and Parker made their dream a reality when the music file-sharing website Napster went online.

Napster was an immediate hit with millennials, who downloaded countless songs from their dorm rooms.

Napster plodded along as a service and website that few people above the age of 25 knew about, until early 2000 when a radio station played a Metallica song before it was even released. It turned out that DJs at the radio station downloaded the song from Napster, so Metallica sued Napster, which led to an out-of-court settlement.

Under normal circumstances, a lawsuit would hurt a company, but it became good publicity for Napster, which saw its number of users surge in late 2000.

But late 2000 also brought more lawsuits for the beleaguered tech company.

The Recording Industry Association of America sued Napster for copyright infringement. Napster's only defense was the First Amendment of the US Constitution, but free speech doesn't necessarily mean you can make money off what other people have said. Or at least, that's what the courts ruled against Napster in 2001.

Napster appealed the decision and lost, forcing the company into bankruptcy and to close down on September 3, 2002.

There's a good chance that if you're under the age of 40, you've never even heard of Napster. The reality is that Napster influenced later filesharing and streaming services, but it was just too far ahead of its time and for that reason, it became one of the greatest failures in modern American tech history.

31

THE FAILURE TO SAVE
THE HOSTAGES

Jimmy Carter is often thought of as a failed president. The Democrat only served one term as America's 39th president, largely due to economic problems, but there was also the idea that he was weak. In fairness to Carter, he probably was a genuinely nice guy, too nice to be the president. He failed to come down tough on his enemies when he needed to and when he tried, it ended in epic failure.

The biggest failure of Carter's presidency was Operation Eagle Claw, which was a mission that took place on April 24-25 to rescue American hostages in Iran. After the failure of Eagle Claw, Carter's loss to Reagan in the 1980 presidential election was all but assured.

Carter's presidency was tough from the beginning. He was inheriting a mess from the Watergate scandal and the economy was quite weak, to say the least, but his biggest challenge came when Iran had a revolution that replaced the pro-American Shah with a militant Islamic theocracy.

But as bad as that was, things got much worse when militant Iranian students took over the US embassy on November 4, 1979, and held 52 Americans hostage.

The Iran Hostage Crisis, as it became known, put America and the world on edge and proved to be a major liability for Carter.

Carter was under immense pressure. The longer he waited, the greater the chance some of the hostages would die. He also didn't need the crisis being used against him in the upcoming presidential election, so he got together with his military and political advisors to formulate a rescue plan they called Operation Eagle Claw.

Operation Eagle Claw was to be as ambitious a plan as its name was confidence-inspiring, involving all the branches of the military and the CIA. Eight helicopters would rendezvous with C-130 transport planes in an isolated salt flat in southeastern Iran, where the helicopters would refuel and continue to a second location outside the capital city of Iran, Tehran.

The assault team would be comprised of 132 members of the elite Delta Force and Army Rangers. The Delta Force members were to take the embassy, rescue the hostages, and then meet up with CIA members who would lead them to an airfield the Rangers had secured.

It all sounds pretty cool, like something out of a Tom Clancy novel, right? Well, notice the keyword I used was "would." This very ambitious rescue plan failed as it got off the ground...literally!

A severe dust storm on the night of April 24, 1980, hampered the first phase of Eagle Claw, and some intangible conditions on the ground didn't help either. A bus full of Iranian civilians was parked on what the Americans planned to use as their improvised landing strip, so they had to be detained while the operation was taking place.

Then a fuel tanker full of contraband fuel showed up, and when it wouldn't stop, an American soldier fired a hand-held rocket into it, killing the passenger and starting a big fire.

When the fiasco on the ground was finally cleared, it turned out that the dust storm had taken out three of the eight helicopters. Two returned to Navy aircraft carriers in the Persian Gulf before reaching the rendezvous and one that did reach the rendezvous was determined to be not fully operational.

With only five helicopters able to continue to the second rendezvous, the order was given to abort the mission, but the helicopters in the field still needed to refuel before returning to the carrier.

As the planes were refueling the helicopters, one of the copters hit a plane, causing a crash and eight deaths.

The rest of the helicopters were able to safely refuel and limp back to the carrier.

When news of the failed mission was announced, it was vindication to the Islamists in Iran that God was on their side, while Americans were left demoralized and scratching their heads. Reagan went on to beat Carter in a landslide, and all the hostages were released on the day of his inauguration.

If Operation Eagle Claw had been successful, it would be remembered as one of the most daring rescue missions in world history. There's also a good chance it would've gained Carter a second term in the White House.

Instead, Operation Eagle Claw proved to be one of the biggest failures in US military history, and it helped ensure that Jimmy Carter's presidency would be remembered by many as a failure.

32

EPIC FRAUD AND EPIC FAIL

In late 2000 and early 2001, the US experienced a brief recession. In terms of recessions, it was relatively minor, although you probably didn't think that at the time if you were invested in one of the many tech companies that went belly up. As one tech company after another went bankrupt in what is now known as the bursting of the dot com bubble, the bankruptcy of one non-tech company caught headlines: Enron.

Enron was an energy giant that was worth more than $100 billion at its peak, and the Texas-based corporation was known to most in the industry as a reputable company and a good place to invest.

But then in 2001, it was revealed that although Enron may once have been a successful company, built on ethical business practices, it had devolved into a cesspool of corruption and greed. When the company's executives filed Chapter 11 bankruptcy on December 2, 2001, which was the largest bankruptcy in American history until the Lehman Brothers, it opened the books revealing how corrupt and what a failure of a company Enron was.

But it wasn't always that way and didn't have to end up that way either.

Enron became a company when two energy companies, InterNorth and Houston Natural Gas, merged in 1985. Houston Natural Gas CEO Kenneth Lay would become Enron's first and only CEO and chairman, leading the corporation to fame and huge profits, but also eventually to infamy, corruption, and the dustbin of history.

Enron did well throughout the 1990s, but as it was later revealed, that was partly because the company's accountants skirted some tax laws and went into some pretty gray territory.

Although the accounting practices may have been technically legal, once their details were made public, investor confidence in the company dropped. The reality of Enron's even shadier and illegal practices was also revealed. It turns out that Enron executives were making business deals with limited partnerships owned by Enron. This arrangement meant that Enron could dump funds into these limited partnerships to make them look profitable or take money out of them and back into Enron to hide true losses.

In other words, Enron executives were playing a shell game.

But as bad as the shell game and shady accounting practices were, they were nothing compared to the insider trading going on at Enron.

As Enron's stock soared to over $90 in the summer of 2000, it dropped to less than half of that a year later. Some thought Enron's stock was overvalued and was undergoing a normal cyclical correction, but in fact, plenty of insider trading was happening.

The worst part about this whole failure is that Lay kept telling investors to buy Enron as he and his wife sold their shares worth tens of millions.

The economic and legal fallout of the Enron failure was catastrophic.

Several top Enron executives were charged and convicted of various felonies and given sentences ranging from probation to prison. Lay was set to be sentenced for his part in the fraud when he unexpectedly died of a heart attack in 2006.

The Arthur Andersen accounting firm, which Enron used to do their books, was brought down by the scandal, and of course, investors lost millions.

The corrupt actions of Kenneth Lay and his executives at Enron will forever be remembered as one of the worst corporate fails in American history and a cautionary tale to anyone who thinks "cooking the books" is a good idea. The IRS is watching and although they may not get you tomorrow or even next year, chances are they'll come knocking at your door eventually.

33

A FORCE OF NATURE AND FAILURE OF LEADERS

When Hurricane Katrina made landfall at Buras-Triumph, Louisiana, on August 29, 2005, it was a Category 3 hurricane. Few people thought that it would do the damage it eventually did, killing more than 1,800 people when flooding overtook the New Orleans area. But they should've been better prepared because as powerful as Hurricane Katrina may have been, it wasn't the strongest hurricane to make landfall in the US.

The thing that made Katrina such a tragedy was the reaction, or inaction, by government leaders. As leaders failed to react quickly enough, more people were killed, and fingers began being pointed. In the end, to the people who survived the ordeal, help never came quick enough and when it did, it often wasn't enough. For them, Katrina was a failure in leadership more than anything.

As Katrina was bearing down on Louisiana, the state's governor, Kathleen Blanco stated confidently on August 27 that "I believe we are prepared. That's the one thing that I've always been able to brag about."

It was soon revealed that Blanco had nothing to brag about.

To her credit, Blanco did realize the situation was probably going to get much worse than it already had, so she requested funds and assistance from US President George W. Bush and the federal government.

But things move slowly in the government, so Blanco was forced to begin evacuations on her own and appeal to neighboring states' governors for additional national guard troops.

The real failure in leadership was with New Orleans mayor Ray Nagin. According to the US's National Response Plan, in the event of an emergency, local officials take immediate responsibility and are then supported by state and federal officials. In the case of Hurricane Katrina, Mayor Nagin showed an utter lack of leadership. First, he rejected an offer by Amtrack to help evacuate the city's residents and then he refused to order a mandatory evacuation. When Nagin finally did order a mandatory evacuation on August 28, many thought it was too little too late. Finally, just before Katrina hit, Nagin flew with his family to Dallas to wait it out.

How's that for a shepherd of the people?

Nagin later blamed state and federal leaders for the problems in New Orleans, despite Blanco doing relatively well after her initial misstatement and Bush sending federal troops and funds to the area.

With that said, their hands weren't clean in the tragedy.

Blanco should've prepared the state better and the failure of the levees was a federal problem. Also, the organizational issues certainly could've been handled better by the feds and Bush, who as the president had the final say and ability to make things happen.

In the end, the tragedy essentially forced Blanco out of office, as she didn't seek re-election in 2007. And although Nagin did narrowly win re-election in 2006, he was later convicted of fraud and bribery while he was in office and was sentenced to 14 years in prison in 2014.

Nagin may have thought he wiggled out from his failure during Katrina in 2006, but sometimes life has a way of enacting cosmic justice.

34

THE ATARI 5200: GREAT IDEA, FAILED EXECUTION

In 1981, Atari was high on top of the home video game world. Its Atari 2600 console was the most popular home system by far, which was due to its large library of games and some pretty good marketing. But things change fast in the gaming and home computer industries, and by the end of that year, Atari was facing some pretty stiff competition.

The emergence of home computers made by companies such as Apple and Texas Instruments signaled to Atari that they should get into that field of computers. The reality was, though, that Atari was better suited for the home video game console system market.

Atari's foray into the home computer market could be described at best - as unspectacular and at worst a failure.

So, Atari went back to what it knew, but it also had growing competition in that market as well. The Intellivision home video game system proved to be a capable high-end alternative to the 2600 and the ColecoVision system, which came out in August 1982, quickly made a splash in the industry with its new style of controllers and the first home version of what would become the classic *Donkey Kong* video game.

In response, Atari introduced its new console system, the 5200, in 1982. The 5200 proved to be as big a failure as the E.T. game and was another reason why Atari lapsed into obscurity as a gaming company in the early 1980s.

Atari released the 5200 in 1982 with a major marketing blitz, but when gamers brought the system home, they immediately recognized it was ripping off the ColecoVision in many ways. Fair enough, the ColecoVision was a successful, high-selling system so taking some "inspiration" from it seemed logical.

But once gamers began playing the 5200, it was immediately clear that it was not ColecoVision.

The 5200 *sucked*.

Perhaps the biggest problem with the 5200 was its complicated and very counter-intuitive controllers. The controllers looked simple enough - they consisted of a joystick and numeric keypad - but once you started playing, you saw how complex they were. Each game came with a plastic overlay card that was placed on the controller. The card would tell the player the function of each number on the numeric keypad of the controller for that particular game. The movement of the controllers also often didn't coincide with the movement of the player's character on the screen.

The graphics on 5200 games were good for the era, but there weren't that many 5200 games available. The Atari 5200 was also unable to play 2600 games and most consumers weren't too keen on running out to buy a new system that had few games to play, especially when those games were so expensive.

The final blow to the 5200 came when the video game crash of 1983 happened. The market collapsed due to an oversaturation of games and console systems, although in the case of the 5200, it could be a chicken or the egg scenario. The 5200 may have played a role in the video game crash, or its demise may have been at least partially due to it.

Either way, the Atari 5200 was an epic gaming failure that set the company back several years. Only one million units were sold before it was discontinued in 1984.

35

JOSEPH HAZELWOOD
AND THE INFAMY OF
THE *EXXON VALDEZ*

Joseph Hazelwood grew up on Long Island in the 1950s and
'60s, watching ships come in and out of the country.
Hazelwood was so drawn to the sea that he joined the Sea
Scouts (a nautical-focused branch of the Boy Scouts) as a boy
and became a seasoned sailor before he even graduated high
school.

Hazelwood took his love of the sea with him to college,
earning a BA in marine transportation from State University of
New York Maritime College in 1968 and then going on to a
successful and lucrative career in commercial shipping. He
worked most of his life for the Exxon corporation, sailing ships
full of oil across the world, and even became the company's
youngest captain at the age of 32.

Everything was going great for Hazelwood until a routine trip
turned into one of the biggest environmental and shipping
failures in American history.

It all happened on the night of March 24, 1989. Hazelwood was captaining the *Exxon Valdez* oil tanker from Alaska to California. After having dinner with some of his crew, Hazelwood went to sleep for the night and left his third mate to navigate through Prince William Sound.

It was a routine journey that Hazelwood and most of the crew of the *Valdez* had done plenty of times prior, but several things came together to create the perfect storm of failure.

The *Valdez* hit a reef just after midnight, which quickly woke Hazelwood and the rest of the crew. Although Hazelwood and the others jumped into action, there was little they could do once the damage had been done.

The *Valdez* lost nearly 11 million gallons of the 53.1 million gallons of oil it was carrying before the ship's breach was sealed and it was hauled to port. As the country watched the developing disaster on television, it was clear that it was going to be one of the worst, if not *the* worst, environmental disasters in American history.

The spilt oil affected more than 1,300 miles of the pristine Alaskan coastline, hurting the local economy and killing thousands of animals. Up to 250,000 seabirds, 247 bald eagles, and 22 killer whales were immediately killed from the spill.

The *Exxon Valdez* disaster still ranks as the second-largest oil spill in terms of total volume and is considered to be the worst in environmental impact.

As the disaster was unfolding, Americans began asking Exxon some pretty serious questions, and Exxon responded by throwing Hazelwood under the bus. Exxon fired him and then the State of Alaska charged him with the felony of second-degree criminal mischief. They claimed he was drunk when the accident happened.

Hazelwood would be found not guilty in 1990.

History has been a bit kinder to Hazelwood, with most scholars stating that the true fault in the disaster is with Exxon.

Exxon had routinely overworked its crews and pushed them when they were tired, which was the case with the *Valdez*. Most importantly, Exxon failed to keep the *Valdez*'s anti-collision technology up to date. When that was combined with a tired, inexperienced third mate, trouble was bound to happen.

But other factors were also primarily the fault of Exxon.

The ship was under-resourced with equipment that could have limited the spill, and the *Valdez* was not tracked by the Coast Guard when it entered the reef.

Exxon's failure destroyed thousands of miles of the delicate ecosystem in Alaska and all but ruined the otherwise stellar sailing career of Joseph Hazelwood. Exxon paid more than $2 billion in out-of-pocket expenses for cleanup, another $1 billion to settle criminal and civil charges, and was ordered to pay more than $500 million in punitive damages (it was originally $5 billion but was later reduced by the Supreme Court).

But don't cry for Exxon; they're still in the business of moving oil out of Alaska.

36

A PERENNIALLY FAILED
PRESIDENTIAL CANDIDATE

Earlier we talked about how the US government is essentially a two-party system, which makes it difficult for third parties to even exist, never mind be successful. If third parties are successful, as the Republicans and Whigs were in the 1800s, they usually supplant one of the two existing parties.

Because of this, attempts at taking power by a specific third party or person affiliated with a third usually only happen occasionally.

But this rule doesn't apply to Lyndon LaRouche.

Lyndon LaRouche was a professional activist who is tied with Harold Stassen for the most presidential campaigns at eight. Unlike Stassen, who was a mainstream member of the Republican Party, LaRouche was anything but mainstream or normal. LaRouche's political platforms, if you could call them that, freely mixed some of the most extreme ideas of the left and right wings of the political spectrum, along with plenty of conspiracy theories about the Illuminati, the royals, aliens, Zionists, and just about anything else you can think of.

Although LaRouche spent time in federal prison from 1989 to 1994 for fraud, it didn't stop him from launching more failed political campaigns. In fact, the only sure thing in American politics from 1976 to 2004 was that there were two parties — the Democrats and Republicans - and that Lyndon LaRouche would run for president and fail miserably in the process.

Lyndon LaRouche was born in 1922 to a Quaker family in New Hampshire. LaRouche's religious affiliation kept him from seeing combat during World War II, although he did serve overseas in support roles.

When LaRouche returned to the United States after the war, he did as most GIs did: he married, started a family, and got a steady job, in his case, working as a management consultant. But as he did the nine-to-five thing, LaRouche slowly began drifting into left-wing politics, which was at least partially spurred by his first wife, Janice Neuberger.

Although he was definitely a bit of an old guy on the New Left scene of the 1960s, LaRouche made contacts with most of the leaders and in 1968 formed the National Caucus of Labor Committees (NCLC) as an umbrella organization of New Left groups.

By the '70s, though, the NCLC took a bizarre and sometimes violent turn. LaRouche began to use the organization more and more as an intelligence apparatus, though to what end it was never made clear. His members also began assaulting members of other New Left groups and the overall direction of the NCLC began veering more right-wing and grafting conspiracy theories to its platform.

It was also in 1976 that LaRouche launched the first of his eight failed campaigns for president.

In 1976, LaRouche founded his own political party - the U.S. Labor Party - to get his foot in the door of the two-party system, but he only got 40,043 votes. LaRouche's later presidential runs were under the banners of the National Democratic Policy Committee and the Independent Democrats for LaRouche, as well as attempts to win the Democrat nomination in the Democratic Party primaries.

Running for president became such a normal thing for LaRouche that he even did so from behind bars for the 1992 presidential election.

Lyndon LaRouche faded from the public eye in the mid-2000s, but he will be forever remembered for his many strange ideas and ability to fail time and time again in his quest to gain the highest office in the land.

37

GEORGE WASHINGTON, WAR CRIMINAL?

As fun, as it's been to laugh at some of the most epic, fails in American history, the truth is that anyone can be the victim of a big fail. Even America's first president, the father of the country, wasn't perfect. He committed an epic fail long before he was president or even general of the Continental Army during the American Revolution.

It was a major fail that almost cost him his military career, which could've meant - well, who knows how history would've changed? So, let's take a look at Washington's big fail.

As you probably know, George Washington grew up on a plantation in Virginia when that State was still a British colony. He had a good life by his era's standards. He actually had a good life by any era's standards, but as much as he may have been privileged, he was also grateful.

When Washington was 31, he joined the Virginia Colonial Militia, eventually getting promoted to second in command.

Washington and his men were sent to what is now Pennsylvania to keep an eye on the French in the area and to make alliances with some of the local Indian tribes. In April 1754, Washington and his regiment of about 300 Virginians met with the Mingo Indian Chief Tanacharison.

The first part of Washington's mission went well.

Tanacharison and some of his braves agreed to travel with the British, but it wasn't exactly clear what they were supposed to do next. You see, the British and the French weren't at war *yet*, but any little thing could set off either side. And with the inexperienced Washington marching with a bunch of inexperienced farm boys from Virginia through what was known at the time as the Northwest Territory, anything could happen.

Washington learned through his Indian allies that a French force led by Joseph Coulon de Jumonville was camped nearby, which could be either an opportunity or a problem for the young officer.

What happened next has been a source of debate for more than 250 years, although whatever happened demonstrated a failure in leadership on Washington's part.

One scenario is that Washington, perhaps given faulty intelligence by his Indian allies who hated the French, was told the French force was much larger than it was and that they were planning an attack. The Virginians and their Indian allies did a preemptive attack, killing all the French, including those who attempted to surrender.

The other scenario is that there was a brief battle between the Virginians and the French, with the French eventually surrendering. Jumonville was treated well by Washington according to the rules of war at the time, but for some reason,

Tanacharison killed him with a tomahawk. The killing then sparked Tanacharison's braves to kill the remainder of the prisoners.

Either way, Washington knew there would be significant fallout from the "battle," so he ordered his men to hastily build a fort at the spot, which became known as Fort Necessity.

Tanacharison and his men weren't having any of it, though, and left.

The Virginians held out for a while but surrendered it on July 3.

The French briefly held the Virginians before letting them return to their homes, but before Washington was allowed to leave, he had to sign a document whereby he admitted to assassinating Jumonville. In other words, George Washington admitted to being a war criminal.

The fallout from Washington's fiasco could immediately be felt around the world.

The British press portrayed Washington as a country bumpkin with no concept of how a civilized war should be fought, and the French were furious that he was allowed to walk away unpunished for what became known as the "Jumonville Affair."

Washington's failed expedition to the Northwest is also thought of as the final event that started the French and Indian War (1754-1763), which was really just the North American theater of the worldwide Seven Years' War (1756-1763).

That was certainly a failure that George Washington would've like to have forgotten. For the most part, it was - after he became the victorious general in the American Revolution and America's founding father.

38

FRANK COLLIN: FAILED JEWISH NEO-NAZI

Modern society can be pretty confusing at times. With social and technological changes happening every day right before our eyes, problems are inevitable. Many people have a difficult time fitting in and finding out where their place is in all of this.

Some people turn to drugs and alcohol to deal with feelings of displacement, while others dive into sex or criminal behavior.

As for native Chicagoan Frank Collin, he turned to extreme politics.

Turning to extreme politics - left or right-wing - during times of great change is actually quite common in modern times. But what makes the case of Frank Collin so bizarre is that he was of Jewish ancestry, yet he became a high-profile professional neo-Nazi in the 1970s.

Maybe it was the act of ultimate rebellion by Collin, a man who never really did much with his life, but in the end, it proved to be one big fail.

Frank Collin was born in 1944 in Chicago and raised in a white ethnic neighborhood of the city, attending Catholic schools. His mother was a devout Catholic, but his father was a non-practicing Jew who was born Max Cohn in Germany. Cohn had changed his name to Collin after emigrating from Germany to sound more American.

Frank was an average student and while attending South Illinois University in the far southern part of Illinois, he got homesick, so he dropped out and returned to Chicago.

But the Chicago of the 1960s was a very different place from the one Collin grew up in as a boy.

The city's ethnic Polish, German, Italian, and Irish neighborhoods were shrinking, with those people moving to the suburbs. In their place came new Hispanic immigrants and Blacks from other neighborhoods as well as from the Southern states. By the late 1960s, as civil rights marches were happening across the country, many neighborhoods in Chicago were becoming hotbeds of racial violence, with White, Black, and Hispanic gangs fighting over turf.

As this was all happening, Collin joined the American Nazi Party. Collin was a good soldier, taking part in demonstrations and other activities, and although he wasn't afraid to mix it up in the streets, his primary asset to the Nazis was his ability to organize high-profile events in Chicago.

So, when American Nazi Party founder and leader George Lincoln Rockwell was assassinated in 1967, Collin thought the leadership should pass to him. Instead, it passed to another guy, thanks in part to Collin's father.

Max Collin/Cohn went to the Chicago press with a story about his Jewish ancestry, exposing his son, the potential Fuhrer of the Windy City, as less than Aryan. Collin denied the allegations to his fellow Nazis and although he retained the loyalty of the Chicago Nazis, the national organization decided to go with another leader.

In response, Collin decided to form his own, separate version of the American Nazi Party. And throughout the 1970s, he was relatively successful. Collin was able to win the support of some disaffected young men, and he held several demonstrations in Chicago's Marquette Park.

The highpoint of Collin's Nazi career came in 1977 when he applied for a permit to march through the heavily Jewish suburb of Skokie. The city of Chicago required Collin to post a pricey bond to continue having demonstrations in Marquette Park, so he sued the city with the help of the ACLU. As he waited for the ruling, he turned his eyes toward the suburbs, including Skokie.

The town of Skokie had passed several ordinances that essentially made it impossible for the Nazis to march. So, with the ACLU's help, Collin sued Skokie.

Although Collin won the case against Skokie, it went all the way to the US Supreme Court. He decided to keep marching in Marquette Park when the city of Chicago relented on their stringent requirements.

But for Frank Collin, it was the last victory he would experience.

Not long after his Supreme Court victory, Collin was cast out by his fellow Nazis when they found compromising pictures of him with underage boys at the organization's headquarters. The Nazis contacted the police who promptly arrested Collin for child molestation. He was convicted in 1979 and served three years in the Illinois state prison system.

When Collin was released from prison, he faded into obscurity to be forever remembered as a failed Jewish neo-Nazi.

39

I THOUGHT WE WERE USING METRIC?

Scientists are supposed to be the smartest people in the world, right? They design our computers, engineer our skyscrapers, and save us from diseases. The most brilliant of all scientists even send people and things into outer space.

But even the geniuses among us occasionally fail in some pretty big ways.

On September 23, 1999, scientists from the Jet Propulsion Laboratory in Pasadena, California were anxiously following one of their latest creations, the NASA Mars Climate Orbiter, as it settled into a stable orbit around the Red Planet. The Orbiter was to be the first craft from Earth to observe the weather on another planet. And at the cost of $125 million, it wasn't a cheap project.

But as the scientists watched their computer screens, they lost track of the Orbiter. For some reason, it had burned up in Mars' atmosphere.

The turn of events was a major letdown to everyone involved. All the scientists were sure they had designed a craft that would work, so everyone was perplexed by what happened. Yet, while a few fingers were pointed, many thought it was just one of those hazards of space travel.

Then a NASA review board revealed the failure was completely human and completely avoidable.

It turns out that when the software was written to calculate the amount of force the Orbiter's thrusters would need to exert when entering Mars' atmosphere, it was done in pounds. For whatever reason, the JPL engineers read the measurements in the metric measurement of newtons, which caused the orbiter to be off by just enough for it to be destroyed.

It was an error that should've been caught. Actually, it really wasn't an error at all, as the engineers at Lockheed Martine express force in pounds, while the engineers at JPL do so in newtons. The JPL engineers knew this and apparently assumed the conversion had already been made!

You could say that this major failure was the result of the US's refusal to switch to the metric system, or you could look at it as a case of no matter how smart a person may be, there's always room to fail.

40

EPIC JAPANESE VICTORY WAS ACTUALLY AN EPIC FAIL

On December 7, 1941, the Japanese Empire made the monumental decision to strike first at the United States by attacking the military bases in Pearl Harbor, Hawaii. The attack was a tactical victory for Japan, as more than 2,000 American servicemen were killed, four battleships were sunk, several other ships were severely damaged, and the US Pacific Fleet had its operations severely hampered.

But as you know, the attack also galvanized the American people and set into motion a sleeping giant that eventually out-produced anything the Axis Powers could muster, which eventually helped the Allies win World War II.

So, you could say that the results of the attack on Pearl Harbor were sort of a mixed bag for the Japanese.

But the reality is that they could've been much better for the Japanese and terrible for the Americans.

The Japanese attack on Pearl Harbor came in two separate waves led by bombers and fighter planes launched from six aircraft carriers that were supported by 28 submarines.

As the smoke cleared after the second wave and the survivors dug through the rubble to help each other, most were wondering when the next attack would come. There were still plenty of viable targets for the Japanese to hit; actually, the targets that were left were probably more valuable. In the two attacks, the Japanese left the American fuel and torpedo storage and dry dock facilities, and perhaps most important, the storage oil tanks were untouched.

The tanks held a combined 4.5 million gallons of fuel, which if hit with one well-aimed torpedo, could've sent all the tanks up in flames. Not only would the fire have caused immense destruction, but the loss of fuel would've hampered the American war effort.

American Admiral Chester Nimitz later recalled that if the Japanese had attacked the oil tankers, dry docks, and other port facilities, "it would have prolonged the war another two years."

But they didn't, and the rest, as they say, is history.

So, if the fuel tankers were such an easy and valuable target, why didn't the Japanese hit them, to begin with, or at least in a third wave?

The Japanese clearly wanted to destroy any opposition in the first two attacks, which is why they hit the military facilities. The second wave ended just before 10 a.m. local time, and as it did, Admiral Chuichi Nagumo's subordinates urged him to order a third attack. The other Japanese commanders were well aware that the fuel tanks were left unharmed.

But Nagumo ordered the fleet to return to Japanese-held waters.

Whether Nagumo ordered the retreat because his planes were low on fuel or because he believed the objective had been successfully carried out may never be known. But what is known, though, is that by leaving the fuel tanks at Pearl Harbor untouched, the Japanese turned what was at face value a major victory into a major fail.

41

THIS HALL OF FAME FOOTBALL PLAYER SCORED POINTS FOR THE OTHER TEAM

Earlier in this book, we met NFL football player Jim Marshall, who became famous for being one of the Minnesota Vikings' Purple People Eaters of the late 1960s and 1970s. Marshall's gritty style of play earned him the love of fans and the respect - and often fear - of his opponents.

But there was one play Marshall did that earned him plenty of laughs because it was one of professional football's most epic fails.

In 1964, the Minnesota Vikings were still an expansion team that was struggling for wins and identity under coach Norm Van Brocklin, but were slowly turning the corner. The Vikings ended up with a winning record that season, and their identity as a rough and tough team became more pronounced under players like defensive end Jim Marshall.

When the ball was snapped, Marshall was everywhere. He was particularly known for sacking the quarterback and causing and recovering fumbles. Marshall recovered a NFL record of 30 fumbles during his career, which is also how he committed the biggest fail of his career.

On October 25, 1964, the Vikings were in a tight game with the San Francisco 49ers when Marshall tackled a 49ers receiver who then fumbled the ball. As he had done plenty of other times, he picked the ball up and ran with it for the end zone.

Only he ran for the *Vikings'* end zone.

The hilarious film shows Marshall striding for what he thought would be an easy six points, going into the endzone, and then throwing the ball into the stands in celebration. Marshall's elation was quickly tempered when a 49ers player ran up and patted him on the shoulder.

Marshall had just scored two points for the 49ers.

If you're not familiar with the rules of gridiron football, if the team with the ball is stopped in their own endzone, it's ruled a safety and the other team gets two points. In most cases, the team with the ball is usually on offense and the team getting the two points is on defense, but Marshall threw all that upside down with his failed play.

Despite it being such an epic fail, the Vikings won the game, Marshall went on to have an incredible career, and he also had a good sense of humor about the incident, appearing on plenty of talk shows over the years to have some laughs about it.

42

PANCHO VILLA'S INVASION OF THE USA: FAIL FOR HIM OR THE AMERICANS?

The Mexican Revolution (1910-1920) was a time of great upheaval, violence, and change in America's southern neighbor. The result was a change in Mexico's political and social culture that can still be seen there today and although most Americans know little about it, it did directly affect many Americans.

It was during the Mexican Revolution that famed Mexican revolutionary, Pancho Villa, led a raid across the border into the small town of Columbus, New Mexico. The raid was historically important because it was the first time that an armed force had invaded American soil since the War of 1812.

But the raid didn't go as Villa had planned, as well-armed American citizens chased the revolutionaries away. Yet when the American army chased Villa and his men into Mexico, they too failed to accomplish their mission.

The Mexican Revolution was more like a civil war, as several factions throughout the culturally and geographically diverse nation fought for control of the central government. One of the major factions was the Conventionists, who were led by Emiliano Zapata in the south and Pancho Villa in the north, particularly in the border state of Chihuahua.

The Conventionists were able to take power briefly from 1914 to 1915, but their support among the masses was capricious; the leaders such as Villa really didn't believe it was anything different from the people they overthrew.

Francisco "Pancho" Villa was born into poverty and became a Bandido in his teen years. After the Revolution broke out, Villa joined in and quickly established himself as a charismatic leader. In many ways, Villa's image and legend preceded him. Often pictured mustached wearing a sombrero, with a Bandelier wrapped around his torso, Villa invoked images on both sides of the border of a romantic revolutionary from a bygone era.

But then he led that raid on Columbus.

In March 1916, Pancho and the Conventionists were on the defensive and had just lost a major battle. They were hurting for supplies and needed a quick victory for propaganda purposes, so they looked north to the soft Americans.

Or so they thought.

After doing a failed reconnaissance of the town of Columbus, New Mexico, Villa thought it was unprotected and that his nearly 500-man force would waltz right in and do as they pleased.

In reality, there were nearly 400 American soldiers stationed in the town, led by cavalry Colonel Herbert Jermain Slocum. The military presence in Columbus was there precisely because of Villa and the Revolution just across the border, and the soldiers were augmented by hundreds of citizens with guns who knew how to use them.

After all, New Mexico is in the US, and it's in the West, and Americans at that time, just as today, owned plenty of guns.

So, when Villa's force invaded the town just after 4.00 a.m. on March 9, they faced plenty of resistance; more resistance than they could handle.

Although Villa's men got away with some guns and other supplies, they lost more than 70 of their men. No matter how Villa spun things, it was a major failure for him and the Conventionists.

But not wanting to be outdone by Villa's epic fail, American President Woodrow Wilson ordered a military expedition led by General John "Blackjack" Pershing to invade Mexico and capture Villa.

The "Villa Expedition" as it became known, began on March 14, 1916, with the goal of capturing Villa. The force of more than 10,000 trekked through Chihuahua searching for the elusive revolutionary but never found him. Instead of getting help from Villa's enemies, the Americans encountered resistance everywhere they went.

The expedition ended in failure on February 7, 1917, as Villa was never captured.

In the end, Pancho Villa's invasion of the USA ended up as a massive failure for him, as he never recovered his former status before he was assassinated in 1923; but the US's attempt to capture the wily revolutionary proved to be an equally epic fail.

43

THE HUNT BROTHERS FAILED BID TO CORNER THE SILVER MARKET

Nelson Bunker Hunt, William Herbert Hunt, and Lamar Hunt were three brothers who also happened to be wealthy heirs to a fortune. Their father, H.L. Hunt, was a billionaire who got his start by winning rights to Arkansas and later Texas oil fields in poker games.

Hunt's three sons, who later become known simply as the "Hunt Brothers," went on to work in the family business but also came up with some of their own money-making ideas.

Youngest brother Lamar helped found the American Football League, which later merged with the National Football Leagues (NFL) and became the American Football Conference (AFC) of the NFL.

Nelson and William also worked on some of their own projects, but in the late 1970s, the Hunt Brothers got together on what was one of the most ambitious moves in American economic history - they tried to corner the silver market. The Hunt

Brothers' plan worked well for a while, but a combination of volatility in the market and government intervention brought it all crashing down in one of the biggest, but little-known, big business fails in American history.

The American economy was very volatile in the late '70s, with a rare combination of high-interest rates, high inflation rates, and high unemployment.

In times such as those, many people choose to invest their money in precious metals such as gold and silver, which is exactly what the Hunt Brothers began doing.

The Hunt Brothers began buying up all the silver in the world in the form of physical silver and futures contracts. They used futures contracts to buy up physical silver, which they held in a pool with some Arab investors. In fact, it was estimated the Hunt Brothers owned about one-third of the world's silver supply, which drove the price up from $6.08 a troy ounce (there are just over three grams more in a troy ounce than a standard ounce) in January 1979 to $49.45 a troy ounce in January 1980.

As inflation was devaluing the price of the dollar, the Hunt Brothers cashed in on their futures contracts in physical silver payments instead of dollars, eventually building their silver stock to 200 million troy ounces.

You can probably imagine that the government wasn't too happy with this situation, and neither was the Federal Reserve Bank, which is a form of a government entity. The Federal Reserve raised interest rates, giving more value to the dollar, and the precious metal exchanges set limits on how much silver could be bought or held.

But what truly killed caused the Hunt Brothers' plan to fail was when the Chicago Board of Trade, which is where most commodities futures are traded in the US, raised margins. This combined with the New York Commodities Exchange restricting the purchase of commodities on margin put the Hunt Brothers in a bind.

Since the Hunt Brothers had leveraged so much of their holdings through margins, they found themselves unable to meet their obligations when the price of silver plummeted on March 27, 1980.

The Hunt Brothers owed nearly $2 billion to investment banks and security firms. If they were unable to pay, then it would send a devastating ripple effect through Wall Street that would eventually make its way to Main Street.

Remember "too big to fail?" Well, this was one of the original cases.

So, the Hunt Brothers were floated a credit line of over $1 billion to pay some of these firms, but it didn't keep them from going bankrupt. After a series of lawsuits were leveled against them, the Hunt Brothers filed Chapter 11 Bankruptcy in 1988. They were banned from trading in the commodities market for the remainder of their lives and their family fortune declined through the 1980s.

It should be noted that, despite their major fail in silver, Nelson and Lamar died wealthy men and the still-living William is worth an estimated $2 billion.

Just remember, if you happen to have a couple of billion dollars on hand and are thinking about cornering a precious metals market, remember the major fail of the Hunt Brothers.

44

BOMB MAKING COMPONENTS WERE ONCE SOLD AS A TOY

Yes, you read the correctly, and if you're a boomer reading this, you may remember the toy known as the Gilbert U-238 Atomic Energy Lab, commonly known as the "Atomic Energy Lab." The Atomic Energy Lab was created by inventor Alfred Carlton Gilbert, who became famous and wealthy for inventing the Erector Set.

Gilbert was a true American patriot who believed that toys should edify as well as entertain children. After the success of the Erector Set, he turned his attention to the creation of a laboratory set, a type of toy that was extremely popular in the early 1950s.

To make his lab set original and relevant with the times, Gilbert came up with the idea of a toy that would allow children to learn about atomic science. After all, it was the Atomic Age and American children knowing about atomic science would help them and the country in the future, Gilbert reasoned.

So, the Atomic Energy Lab hit the shelves in 1950.

The lab included a cloud chamber that allowed kids to see alpha particles, a Geiger counter, an electroscope, and a spinthariscope used to view nuclear disintegration. Perhaps the most amazing parts of the set were the four samples of real uranium ores that came from three radiation sources!

And to make sure that kids stay interested, a comic book of the popular Dagwood character of the era was included, titled "Dagwood Slits the Atom!"

The set was marketed as the "Most modern scientific set ever created!" And the advertising also promised that you could "Watch actual atomic disintegration!"

The scary toy was never a big seller and was discontinued as a failure in 1954. If you can find a set today, it'll cost you a hefty price and likely won't have the uranium.

Back in the 1950s, it cost $49.50, which was also quite a hefty price as that would be equivalent to more than $530 today.

It was that steep price that did the Atomic Laboratory in more than anything. Most people in the 1950s really didn't know much about atomic energy or uranium, so the idea didn't really scare anyone, and there are also no known cases where a kid was harmed by the product. We now know, though, that radiation can affect a person over a long period, so there's no telling how many kids were poisoned by the Atomic Energy Laboratory.

45

APPLE REALLY FAILED
WITH THE NEWTON

There's no doubt that Apple has built a loyal following with consumers who swear by their products despite their high prices compared to similar technology. People will pay more and stand in long lines for the latest iPhone, and those who use Macs wouldn't think of buying a "PC" as they somewhat derisively refer to any computer that isn't an Apple.

But Apple hasn't hit a home run with every one of its products.

Way back in the 1990s, as the tech boom was starting to take hold across the world, personal digital assistants (PDAs) were all the rage. PDAs were small, hand-held computers, about the size of smartphones today, which could be used for a variety of office tasks. People used them to compose and keep documents, for scheduling reminders, and some were even able to connect to the internet, although they had to be physically connected to a modem or a computer that was hooked to the net.

Remember, the 1990s was before wireless!

Apple was a very successful company by the early 1990s and was looking to expand its footprint into other areas of the tech market, so when PDAs started becoming popular, Apple went all-in with a $100 million investment in their own device, the Apple Newton.

When the Newton came out in 1993, it was billed as the next great thing in the Computer Age. It had all the features for a new, tech-savvy generation that was on the go and ready to move into the future. For instance, it had a "connection kit" that allowed it to connect to other printers and computers, and therefore, the internet. The Newton also had a touch screen and pen stylus for all those people who hate keyboards. And better yet, the Newton had handwriting recognition that would translate your writing into printed text.

Except it rarely did that and instead become known more for its common typos.

Then there was the fact that it wasn't really a convenient device. At 4.5 x 7 inches and one inch thick and nearly one pound in weight, the Newton wasn't something you could carry in your pocket.

But all of this was worth it, right?

Wrong...The Newton's retail price was $700, which seemed much too high for the average person who saw it as little more than a hi-tech notepad. When Steve Jobs returned to Apple in 1997, he realized what a failure the Newton was and discontinued it. The last Newton sold in 1998.

46

STEVE BARTMAN: VICTIM OF A CURSE OR JUST AN EPIC FAIL?

Many modern sports are very superstitious. Fans and players often go through well-choreographed routines before, during, and after games, which if broken can lead to disastrous results on the field - or so it's believed.

Perhaps the most superstitious of all sports is baseball and of the many superstitions that baseball players and fans believe in, the most unique is the "curse."

We've already seen how the Chicago White Sox believe they were cursed after some players threw the World Series, and later we'll look at how many thought the Boston Red Sox were cursed, but now let's consider the strangest baseball curse of all and how an epic fan fail in 2003 was a part of it.

Just a few miles to the north of where the White Sox play, but light-years away in terms of fan culture, is Wrigley Field, the home of the Chicago Cubs. In 1945, the Cubs already had a storied tradition, but it had been a long time since they had won a World Series title, 1908 to be exact. The Cubbies seemed poised to finally win it all again that year when something really strange, some may even say supernatural, happened at Wrigley Field during game four of the World Series.

A fan named William Sanis, who owned a local bar called the Billy Goat Tavern, decided to bring his bar's mascot, a goat named Murphy into the stadium.

Sanis and his goat were kicked out of the stadium, to which he replied, "them Cubs, they ain't gonna win no more."

The Cubs went on to lose that game and the series, giving rise to the idea of a curse.

There were some close calls in the decades after 1945, but 2003 seemed to be the year the Cubs would finally break the curse. On October 14, they were up three games to two over the Florida Marlins in the National League Divisional Series and were up 3-0 in game six in the eighth inning. Marlins player Louis Castillo hit a routine pop-up foul ball that drifted toward the stands. It would've been an easy, routine out for Cub's outfielder Moisés Alou to make, but suddenly it seemed like out of nowhere a bespeckled Cub's fan wearing a Cubs cap, earphones, and a green turtleneck reached over the wall and took the ball from Alou.

That fan was Chicago area native Steve Bartman.

Castillo was given another chance, drawing a walk. The rest was all downhill for the Cubs who went on to lose the game and the series.

Bartman had to be escorted out of the stadium by security and had to have police protection at his home for some time. The White Sox fans are generally known as the rowdier and tougher of the Chicago baseball fans, but when your team hasn't won the World Series in nearly 100 years, you can get pretty desperate.

Things got so bad for Bartman that the Illinois governor at the time, Rod Blagojevich, who later served prison time for corruption, suggested Bartman check in to the witness protection program.

Many Cubs fans believed Bartman was living proof of the curse of the goat. He avoided interviews and lived in obscurity for the next several years. When the Cubs finally did win the World Series in 2016, the organization offered him a championship ring as a token of their sincerity to move beyond the incident. Bartman briefly reemerged from his self-imposed exile to say that he was glad the Cubs won but graciously refused the offer.

Sports fans will forever argue if the Cubs were truly cursed by a goat or if they were the victims of poor management and underperforming teams. Those who believe in the curse often point to the Steve Bartman incident, but those who are more grounded in the mundane say Bartman was just an over-exuberant fan who ended up committing an epic sports fail.

47

"PRO-STALIN" PROBABLY WASN'T A GOOD CAMPAIGN PLATFORM

You can't blame a guy for admitting when he's wrong. At least, that's what they say, but in the case of former Vice President and Secretary of Commerce, Henry Wallace, his admission that he was wrong about the Soviet Union under Joseph Stalin was too little too late.

For Wallace, coming out in favor of Stalin during the 1948 presidential election proved to be a massive political failure, as big as Lyndon LaRouche's many failed presidential bids or the efforts of any failed third party. This is because it not only brought down his career but those of many of his supporters.

Henry Agard Wallace was born on October 7, 1888, on an Iowa farm. Wallace's family later went into the newspaper business and then politics, as his father Henry served as Secretary of Agriculture under Republican presidents Harding and Coolidge from 1921 through 1924.

Henry followed in his father's footsteps but adopted more left-wing politics. Like his father, he served as the Secretary of Agriculture under Democrat President Franklin Roosevelt from 1933 to 1940 and then as Vice President from 1941 to 1945. After Roosevelt was elected for a fourth term, things got interesting.

Many in the Democrat Party feared that Roosevelt wouldn't live through his fourth term, so they wanted to choose a Vice President who had the best chance of winning and uniting the party. The Southern Democrats at the time were pro-segregation and since Wallace was pro-integration, they threw their support to Henry Truman.

Roosevelt then appointed Wallace as the Secretary of Commerce.

So, there was a bit of bad blood between Wallace and Truman when the 1948 election rolled around.

But what mattered is what the Democrat Party leaders thought and what the American people thought. The party leaders liked Truman, who was tough on communism and moderate on racial issues, versus Wallace who was clearly left-wing on both of those.

Instead of trying to wrest the nomination away from Truman, Wallace decided to run as a third-party candidate under the Progressive Party banner. It's debatable if Wallace really thought he could win, but what isn't debatable is how much of a failure the campaign was.

Wallace was ahead of the curve on some issues such as desegregation - in 1948 that wasn't a popular issue in most places - but he really failed with his support of the Soviet Union.

It was bad enough that he campaigned on closer relations with Joseph Stalin. Yes, Stalin was on the Allies' side in World War II, but by that time, the world knew of the horrors he had subjected the Soviet Union to, especially the Holodomor in Ukraine. Members of the Communist Party USA also worked on Wallace's campaign and more than likely a few Soviet spies infiltrated the organization.

When the election was finally over, Wallace only managed to take 2.4% of the vote, which was actually more than many people thought he'd get.

After the election, Wallace said, "I predict that the Progressive Party will rapidly grow into the dominant party."

No, buddy - the US wasn't quite ready for that brand of leftism.

Wallace's failure in 1948 ruined his career. It also put him and many of his supporters in the crosshairs of investigations during the 1950s Red Scare. Perhaps knowing that he faced investigations or worse for his past cozying up to Stalin and the Soviets, Wallace wrote a 1952 book, *Where I Was Wrong,* where he essentially admitted that his pro-Soviet political career was wrong and a failure.

A person can always change their opinion, but in the case of Henry Wallace, it apparently didn't make up for his political failure because he eventually faded into political obscurity.

48

THIS TV SHOW WAS SO BAD IT WAS CANCELLED MIDWAY THROUGH ITS FIRST EPISODE

Cavemen may have been the biggest TV fail of the 2000s, but our next entry was probably the biggest TV bomb of all time - *Turn-On*.

Following the success of *Rowan & Martin's Laugh-In* during the late 1960s, which mixed counterculture humor with standard American television, the show's producers, Ed Friendly and George Schlatter thought they'd take things farther with a show that was much *more* counterculture and far *less* standard American television. Due to their success, the executives at the ABC network liked the idea and gave the green light for the show to start airing on February 5, 1969.

The ABC executives probably should've thought twice after NBC and CBS rejected the show, but then again, networks routinely pass on hit shows that other networks pick up.

Although *Turn-On* was supposed to be a sketch comedy, nothing about it was like any sketch comedy show before or since. There was no studio audience or laugh track, jump cuts quickly segued one routine to the next, and it mixed live-action, animation, and stop-action in a bizarre mix. And to top it all off, there wasn't a set. All skits were done in front of a white screen!

And the concept was that it was all done in something called a computer.

Not many people knew what a computer was in 1969, which turned out to be another obvious problem of the show.

"The whole idea was to arrest the viewer's attention without having them really comfortable in a place," said Schlatter in a later interview.

That statement clearly shows why *Turn-On* was such a failure.

Outside of possibly film students, no one wants to spend 30 minutes of what would normally be relaxation time getting visually assaulted by a TV screen.

Veteran comedian and TV actor, Tim Conway, who was the only aired episode's first guest host, reminisced.

"George Schlatter thought it was going to be hysterical," Conway said. "And it kind of was, but it was way ahead of its time. I'm not sure that even if you saw it today that maybe that time has also passed."

But Schlatter and company thought they had a winner with their avant-garde product, which they also thought would be bolstered by its bawdy, blue humor. They knew that sex sells, and they thought it would help sell their show.

The thing is, even in 1969, everyone liked a good dirty yarn, but the keyword is *good*. The jokes on *Turn-On* weren't very good and were instead more like something boys would tell each other on the playground during recess.

So, when *Turn-On* began showing on February 5, the viewers immediately called local affiliates to complain. In fact, the local Cleveland affiliate cut the show off after ten minutes and went to a black screen with organ music.

"By the time it got to California it was off," Conway said. "So, we had the coming-out party and the cancellation party, very economical because it was all in one evening, and gone."

And with that, *Turn-On* became the most spectacular failure in American television.

49

THE MANY FAILED MARRIAGES OF LIZ TAYLOR

For those of you reading this who are married, you know it can be a difficult institution, especially since no-fault divorce laws started becoming the law in states across America in the 1970s. By 1979, divorce rates had ballooned to 53% and although they have since gone down a bit, they are still over 40%.

So, with those numbers, it's not uncommon for people to get married once or even twice in a lifetime.

But what about eight times?

This was the case for Hollywood Golden Age starlet, Liz Taylor. Remember her from earlier in this book? Besides being the star of *Cleopatra*, the American A-list actress starred in films, TV shows, and stage productions from the 1940s through the 1980s. Taylor was known for her classical beauty, wide acting range, eccentricity, and many, many lovers.

And when it came to love, Liz was quite unlucky and dare I say, a failure.

Taylor was born to wealthy yet fairly traditional parents who tried to instill their daughter with some of their values even as they promoted her ascent as a teen actor. While Taylor's star was rising, she decided to marry at the age of 18 to Hilton Hotel heir Conrad Hilton Junior. The couple had little in common and divorced after less than a year of marriage.

It would set a pattern for Liz Taylor's lifetime of failed marriages.

Undeterred by her first failed marriage, Taylor wrote it off to youthful inexperience and set her sights on an older, more experienced man. She married British actor Michael Wilding, who was 20 years older than her, in 1952. The marriage was nominally successful, as the couple had two children and it seemed to help both their careers.

But the age difference and different trajectory of their careers - Taylor was becoming an international celebrity while Wilding was barely hanging onto his glory years - led to their divorce in 1957.

Taylor wasted no time after number two. She married film producer Mike Todd about a month later, causing plenty of speculation in the press, but that marriage ended in tragedy about one year later when Todd died in a plane crash.

At this point, most people, no matter how co-dependent they are, would probably get the hint that maybe they just weren't cut out for marriage.

But Liz Taylor wasn't like most people. As I mentioned, she was quite eccentric, converting to Judaism in 1959, which is a religion few convert to other than through marriage. And although Mike Todd was Jewish, as was Taylor's third husband, Eddie Fisher, she later claimed her conversion was authentic and practiced the faith long after her divorce to husband number four.

Oh yeah, Eddie Fisher.

Well, Taylor "stole" singer Eddie Fisher from Debbie Reynolds, which raised more than a few eyebrows.

But if Fisher thought Liz was loyal, he was in for a surprise. In a twist of irony, Taylor left him for her *Cleopatra* co-star Richard Burton. The couple married in 1964 and were *the* celebrity couple of that era. In fact, in many ways, they were the template for later Hollywood power couples like Brad Pitt and Angelina Joline or Nicole Kidman and Tom Cruise. And like those couples, "Liz and Dick," as they were known, were destined to fail.

The couple divorced in 1974.

But Liz and Dick were truly drawn to each other and remarried in 1975, making Burton husband number five and six. By that point, though, Burton had descended into extreme alcoholism and his health was fading, so Taylor dumped him in 1976.

True to form, within months of divorcing Burton for the second time, Taylor met and married Virginia Senator John Warner. In another twist of irony, Taylor became pill and booze addicted, which is why she left Burton both times, leading to her seventh marriage collapsing in 1982.

Taylor was 50 by the time she divorced Warner, and it looked as though she had finally realized she was a failure in marriage. But maybe because she was a true romantic, or possibly not very smart, she married one last time in what was probably the strangest and most eccentric of all her marriages.

In 1991, she married southern California construction worker Larry Fortensky. Maybe it was a case of everything coming full circle, as similar to Taylor's marriage number two, Fortensky was 20 years *her* junior.

The two met at an alcohol and drug treatment center, which should have sent up red flags, and were then married at Michael Jackson's notorious Neverland Ranch.

The couple divorced in 1996, and finally Liz Taylor apparently realized that she was the ultimate failure in marriage because she never gave it another go. Some people may be unlucky in love, but Liz Taylor was an utter failure.

50

A $1.5 BILLION MISTAKE

Earlier we discussed the failure of the 1999 Mars Orbiter. It was a mistake of literally a matter of inches that could have been easily prevented but instead turned into a costly, humiliating failure for all the scientists involved.

For this next failure, let's return to NASA for an even bigger failure — the Hubble Telescope.

When the Hubble Telescope was launched in 1990, NASA described it as the next big step in the unmanned exploration of space. Telescopes had been used in space since the 1960s, but they were onboard rockets: the scientists at NASA wanted a high-powered, permanently orbiting telescope in low orbit.

So, NASA scientists began working on the Hubble, which they named for legendary American astronomer Edwin Hubble (1889-1953).

The Hubble was quite an ambitious project. When the Hubble was finished and launched into space in 1990, it weighed nearly 25,000 pounds, was more than 43 feet long, and its most important part - the mirror - was nearly eight feet in diameter. Driven by solar power, the Hubble could collect more than

40,000 times of light than the human eye and could see more than 13.4 billion light-years away.

With that many bells and whistles, it's no wonder the price tag was $1.5 billion.

So, when the Hubble finally went online on May 20, 1990, NASA scientists waited anxiously for its first images to come back to Earth. To say they were excited would be an understatement. The scientists were about to look at worlds no one had ever seen, but when they received the images, they were less than thrilled.

The pictures looked like something a 1970s Kodak flashcube camera would take, not a Space Age $1.5 billion instrument.

An investigation of the source of the grainy pictures revealed that a testing error during the construction of the lens was the problem. Specifically, the error was a miscalibration that was one-fiftieth the size of a human hair, yet it was big enough to ensure that the pictures coming from space were grainy and low quality.

Since replacing the mirror completely wasn't an option due to its size, a manned mission was sent to the Hubble in 1993 to add five pairs of corrective mirrors known as the Corrective Optics Space Telescope Axial Replacement (COSTAR). COSTAR did the trick, but in the three years that it took to fix the Hubble, the telescope and NASA were the butt of several jokes for their failure, even making an appearance in the film *The Naked Gun 2 ½: The Smell of Fear*.

51

RONALD WAYNE: APPLE COFOUNDER WHO SOLD HIS SHARE FOR $2,300

Despite the Newton, Apple has arguably been the most successful tech company in history. Its home computers revolutionized the way people did business and entertainment in the 1980s, and the iPhone led the way in the smartphone industry in the 2000s.

Apple has also been an extremely successful business, earning its shareholders billions of dollars and spanning its operations across the globe.

You may know that Apple was started in a garage in Los Altos, California in 1976 by Steve Jobs and Steve Wozniak. But did you also know they were joined by a third partner named Ronald Wayne?

Don't feel bad if you don't recognize the name Ronald Wayne because most people don't. He wasn't with the company very long and he's best known for failing to capitalize on its success.

Wayne was a 41-year-old programmer who worked at Atari in 1976, which is where he met the young, bright-eyed Jobs and Wozniak. The two young programmers had some big ideas for building their own computer, so Wayne sort of took them under his wing and became their mentor. Wayne then wrote up a contract for the new business that gave each of the Steves - a 45% share and him 10%.

Not bad for the business behemoth that would become Apple, right?

Well, Wayne didn't quite have the vision of Jobs and Wozniak and had already been burned on previous business deals, so either a few weeks or months later (depending on who tells the story), Wayne sold his 10% of Apple for $800. He then accepted a $1,500 check a year later from Jobs and Wozniak to forgo any claim on Apple's name or intellectual property. So, for helping start the most successful tech company in the world Ronald Wayne cashed in at a cool $2,300...Lol!

End of story, epic fail, right?

Not so fast! As Apple began taking off during the late 1970s, Jobs approached Wayne to rejoin them, but he refused and had the misfortune of watching the company rise to unbelievable heights.

But the final fail came years later when Wayne tried to cash in one last time on his brief ownership of Apple. In the early 1990s, Wayne sold his copy of the contract he signed with Jobs and Wozniak for $500. You probably don't even have to read ahead to know what happened next - the contract later sold at a Sotheby's auction for $1.6 million!

Ronald Wayne may have had a talent for tech, but when it came to business, he only knew how to fail.

52

BILL BUCKNER'S EPIC
WORLD SERIES FAIL

For our last epic American fail, we go back to the superstitious sport of baseball, and you guessed it, another curse.

This supposed curse and fail relates to the Boston Red Sox, whom fans believed were cursed when they sold legend Babe Ruth to their hated rivals, the New York Yankees, in 1920. Ruth and the Yankees would go on the become the "Bronx Bombers" and *the* Major League team of the next two decades, while the Red Sox wallowed in mediocrity for more than 80 years until they won their first World Series since 1918 in 2004.

Die-hard Red Sox fans were sure the World Series drought was the result of the "Curse of the Bambino" as it became known (one of Babe Ruth's nicknames was "the Big Bambino), and could point to numerous chokes and fails by their team as proof.

But no fail was as big as the Red Sox's first baseman's error during game six of the 1986 World Series.

When the Red Sox met the New York Mets in the 1986 World Series, it was one of the most hyped series in recent years. The Mets were a media favorite and even made a music video, while the Red Sox were led by power hitter Wade Boggs.

The Red Sox established themselves early in the series and looked poised to reverse the curse when they were ahead three games to two heading into game six of the series. Game six was tightly played with the Red Sox ahead 3-2 until the Mets scored a run in the bottom of the 8th inning.

The game then went to extra innings.

After scoring two runs in the top of the 10th inning and leading 5-3, the Red Sox looked poised to break the curse.

But the Mets still had their chance in the bottom of the 10th.

Red Sox relief pitcher Calvin Schiraldi quickly and quietly recorded the first two Mets batters in the bottom of the 10th, but then things got really interesting. The seemingly impossible happened when the Mets scored two runs on two outs.

Red Sox manager John McNamara pulled Schiraldi and put in reliever Bob Stanley to get the final out.

Then Mets batter Mookie Wilson batter hit what normally would have been a routine ground ball to Red Sox first basemen Bill Buckner. The city of Boston was about to erupt in joy as all Buckner had to do was pick it up and either run to first or throw it to Stanley who was covering first.

But instead, the ball took a funny bounce and went right through Buckner's legs.

A pin dropping could've been heard in Boston when that happened. And immediately after the silence, a torrent of colorful language.

As veteran broadcaster Vin Scully, who was calling the game on national television said:

"If one picture is worth a thousand words, you have seen about a million words. But more than that, you have seen an absolutely bizarre finish to game six of the 1986 World Series."

Of course, the Mets went on to win game seven and the World Series, causing Red Sox fans nearly two more decades of misery that was at least partially the result of Bill Buckner's epic fail.

CONCLUSION

I hope you enjoyed *The United States of Epic Fails* and learned a few things along the way. There are a few important things you should take away from this book, the first being that life is short so there's nothing wrong with having a little fun with it!

We all need to take a break from the seriousness of our lives and the world, in general, to have a laugh at some otherwise serious things, which may include a few things we consider "sacred cows." So, whether that means you're a Vikings or Bills fan who can't get over your team's constant championship failures, or maybe you were disappointed with the E.T. video game, laughing about it doesn't hurt.

Laughing about some of these failures helps remind us that no matter who we are, or where we come from, we are all prone to flop from time to time. It's going to happen, so as some of the fails we profile show, sometimes it's just better to admit defeat, laugh, and move on.

Of course, some of the failures we profiled in this book were more serious and not too funny, but that brings us to the second takeaway — failures can happen to anyone, anywhere, and at any time. We should always be on guard to prevent failure, ready to deal with them when they happen, and then possibly learn from the experience.

The reality is, though, that we've all flubbed it up at least a few times in our lives and chances are we'll muck things up a few more before we're dead and buried. So then, the question becomes a matter of how bad we'll fail in the future.

Will our future be standard, run-of-the-mill failures that can be dealt with easily, or will we commit an epic failure - or failures - so bad that it will be included in the next volume of *Epic Fails*?

Try not to think about it too hard, though.

Made in United States
North Haven, CT
10 December 2023

45473954R00095